10/10

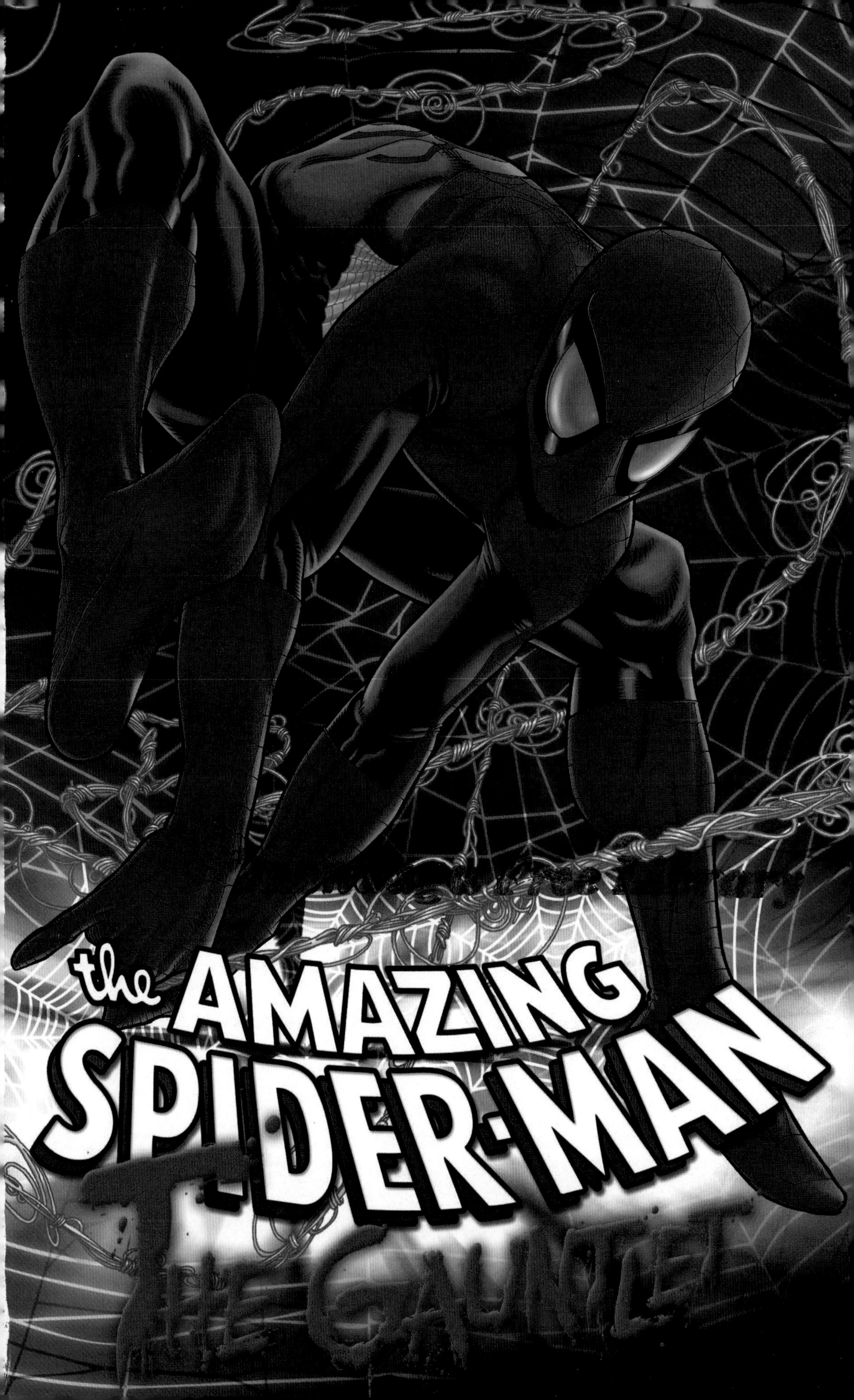
the AMAZING SPIDER-MAN
THE GAUNTLET

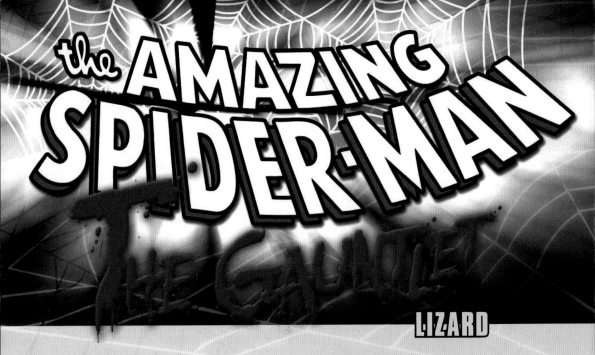

the AMAZING SPIDER-MAN

THE GAUNTLET

LIZARD

GAUNTLET ORIGINS: LIZARD

Writer: **FRED VAN LENTE**
Artist: **JEFTE PALO**
Colorist: **JAVIER RODRIGUEZ**
Letterer: **VC'S JOE CARAMAGNA**

SHED: PRELUDE

Writer: **ROGER STERN**
Artist: **XURXO PENALTA**
Colorist: **MATT HOLLINGSWORTH**
Letterer: **JARED K. FLETCHER**

SHED PROLOGUE

Writer: **ZEB WELLS**
Artist: **CHRIS BACHALO**
Letterer: **VC'S JOE CARAMAGNA**

ISSUES #630-633

Writer: **ZEB WELLS**
Pencilers: **CHRIS BACHALO & EMMA RIOS**
Inkers: **TIM TOWNSEND, JAIME MENDOZA, VICTOR OLAZABA, MARK IRWIN, CHRIS BACHALO & EMMA RIOS**
Colorist: **ANTONIO FABELA**
Letterer: **VC'S JOE CARAMAGNA**

Web-Heads: **BOB GALE, JOE KELLY, DAN SLOTT, FRED VAN LENTE, MARK WAID & ZEB WELLS**
Assistant Editor: **THOMAS BRENNAN** • Editor: **STEPHEN WACKER** • Executive Editor: **TOM BREVOORT**

Collection Editor: **JENNIFER GRÜNWALD** • Editorial Assistants: **JAMES EMMETT & JOE HOCHSTEIN**
Assistant Editors: **ALEX STARBUCK & NELSON RIBEIRO** • Editor, Special Projects: **MARK D. BEAZLEY**
Senior Editor, Special Projects: **JEFF YOUNGQUIST** • Senior Vice President of Sales: **DAVID GABRIEL**

Editor in Chief: **JOE QUESADA** • Publisher: **DAN BUCKLEY** • Executive Producer: **ALAN FINE**

SPIDER-MAN: THE GAUNTLET VOL. 5 — LIZARD. Contains material originally published in magazine form as WEB OF SPIDER-MAN #6 and AMAZING SPIDER-MAN #629-633. First printing 2010. Hardcover ISBN# 978-0-7851-4615-5. Softcover ISBN# 978-0-7851-4616-2. Published by MARVEL WORLDWIDE, INC., a subsidiary of MARVEL ENTERTAINMENT, LLC. OFFICE OF PUBLICATION: 417 5th Avenue, New York, NY 10016. Hardcover: $19.99 per copy in the U.S. and $22.50 in Canada (GST #R127032852). Softcover: $14.99 per copy in the U.S. and $16.99 in Canada (GST #R127032852). Canadian Agreement #40668537. **Printed in the U.S.A.** ALAN FINE, EVP - Office of the President, Marvel Worldwide, Inc. and EVP & CMO Marvel Characters B.V.; DAN BUCKLEY, Chief Executive Officer and Publisher - Print, Animation & Digital Media; JIM SOKOLOWSKI, Chief Operating Officer; DAVID GABRIEL, SVP of Publishing Sales & Circulation; DAVID BOGART, SVP of Business Affairs & Talent Management; MICHAEL PASCIULLO, VP Merchandising & Communications; JIM O'KEEFE, VP of Operations & Logistics; DAN CARR, Executive Director of Publishing Technology; JUSTIN F. GABRIE, Director of Publishing & Editorial Operations; SUSAN CRESPI, Editorial Operations Manager; ALEX MORALES, Publishing Operations Manager; STAN LEE, Chairman Emeritus. For information regarding advertising in Marvel Comics or on Marvel.com, please contact Ron Stern, VP of Business Development, at rstern@marvel.com. For Marvel subscription inquiries, please call 800-217-9158. **Manufactured between 8/2/10 and 9/1/10 (hardcover), and 8/2/10 and 1/26/11 (softcover), by R.R. DONNELLEY, INC., SALEM, VA, USA.**

10 9 8 7 6 5 4 3 2 1

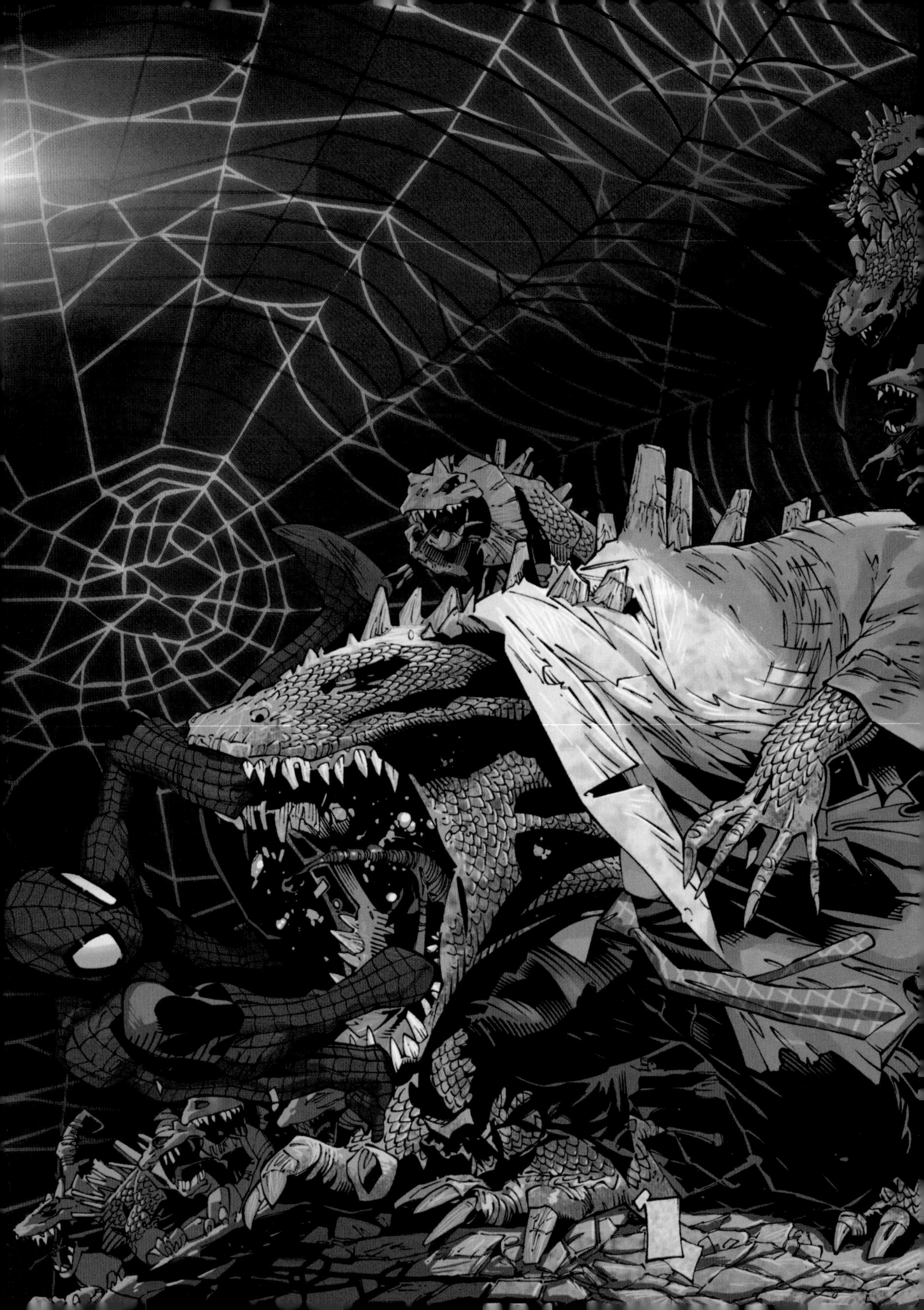

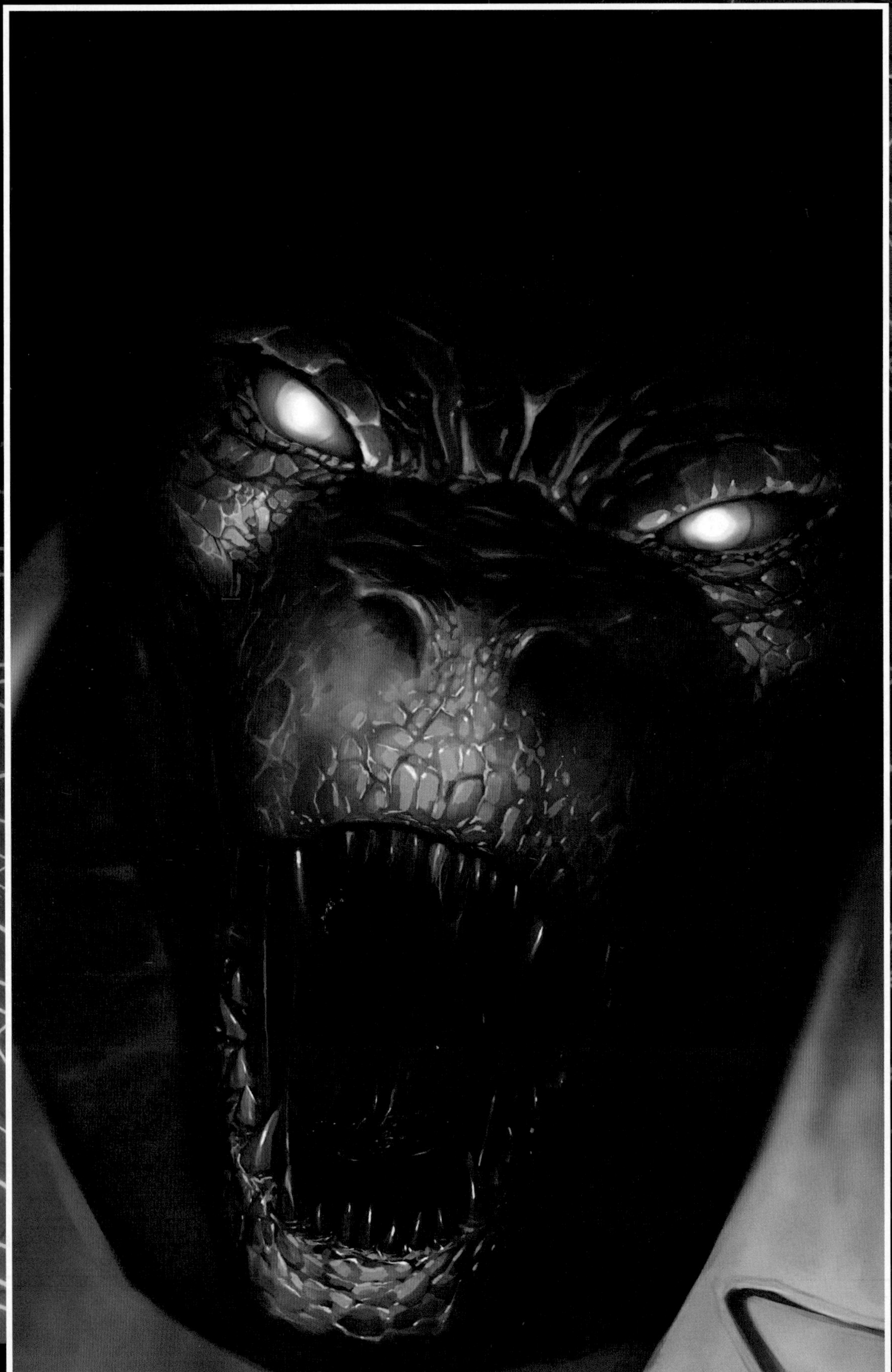

WEB OF SPIDER-MAN #6 – "GAUNTLET ORIGINS: LIZARD" & "SHED PRELUDE" COVER BY JELENA KEVIC DJURDJEVIC

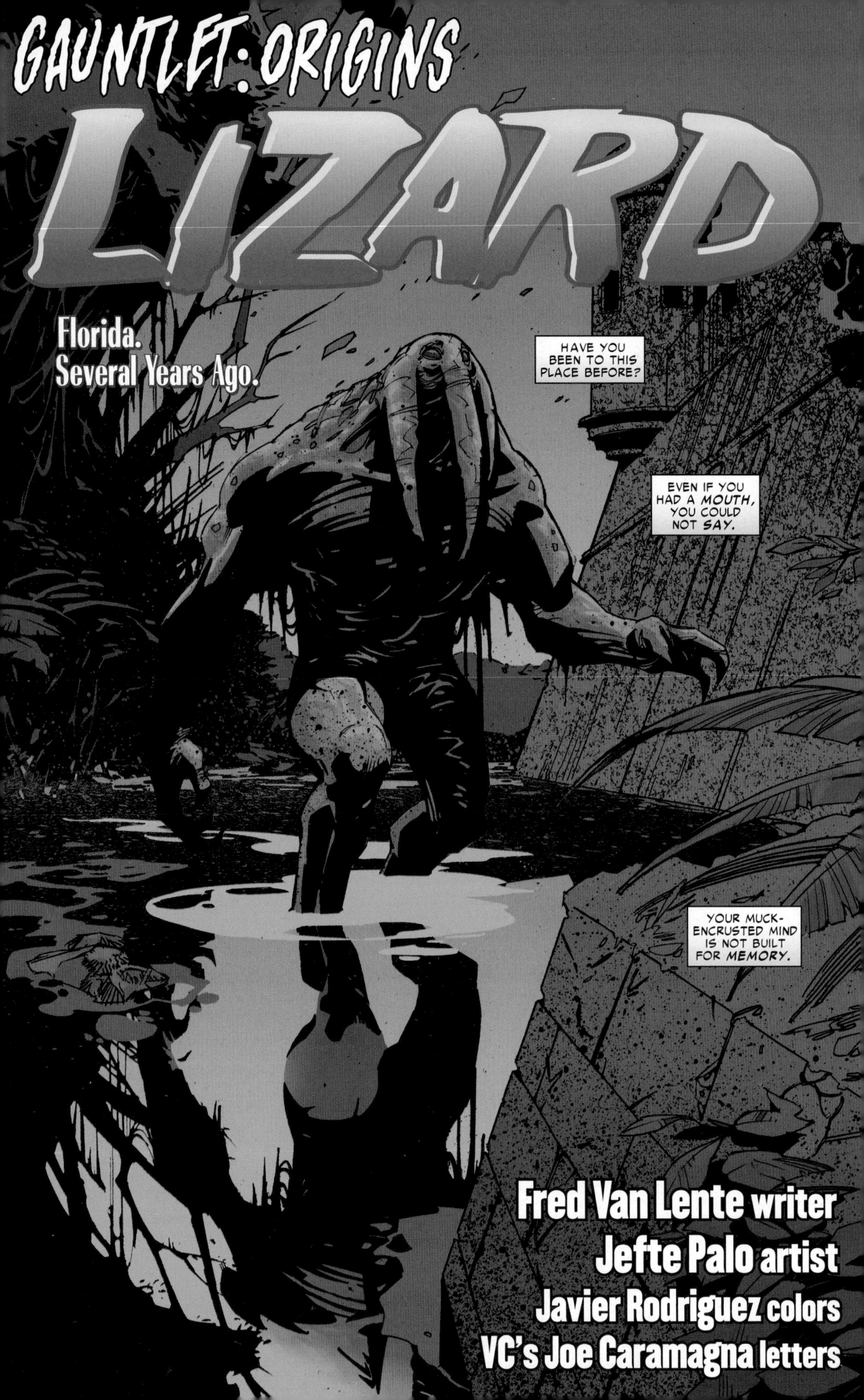
GAUNTLET: ORIGINS
LIZARD
Florida. Several Years Ago.
HAVE YOU BEEN TO THIS PLACE BEFORE?
EVEN IF YOU HAD A MOUTH, YOU COULD NOT SAY.
YOUR MUCK-ENCRUSTED MIND IS NOT BUILT FOR MEMORY.
Fred Van Lente writer
Jefte Palo artist
Javier Rodriguez colors
VC's Joe Caramagna letters

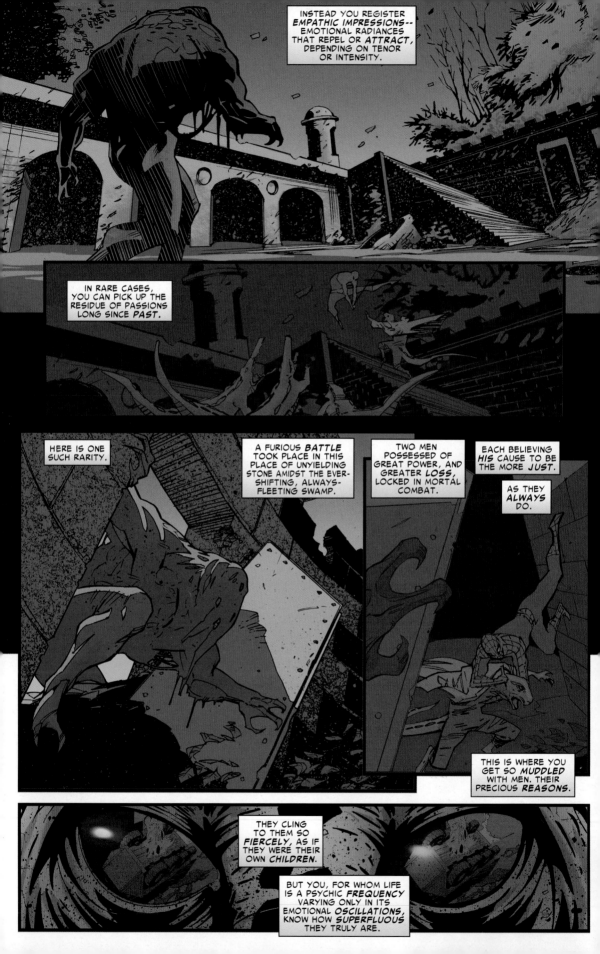

INSTEAD YOU REGISTER *EMPATHIC IMPRESSIONS--* EMOTIONAL RADIANCES THAT REPEL OR *ATTRACT,* DEPENDING ON TENOR OR INTENSITY.

IN RARE CASES, YOU CAN PICK UP THE RESIDUE OF PASSIONS LONG SINCE *PAST.*

HERE IS ONE SUCH RARITY.

A FURIOUS *BATTLE* TOOK PLACE IN THIS PLACE OF UNYIELDING STONE AMIDST THE EVER-SHIFTING, ALWAYS-FLEETING SWAMP.

TWO MEN POSSESSED OF GREAT POWER, AND GREATER *LOSS,* LOCKED IN MORTAL COMBAT.

EACH BELIEVING *HIS* CAUSE TO BE THE MORE *JUST.*

AS THEY *ALWAYS* DO.

THIS IS WHERE YOU GET SO *MUDDLED* WITH MEN. THEIR PRECIOUS *REASONS.*

THEY CLING TO THEM SO *FIERCELY,* AS IF THEY WERE THEIR OWN *CHILDREN.*

BUT YOU, FOR WHOM LIFE IS A PSYCHIC *FREQUENCY* VARYING ONLY IN ITS EMOTIONAL *OSCILLATIONS,* KNOW HOW *SUPERFLUOUS* THEY TRULY ARE.

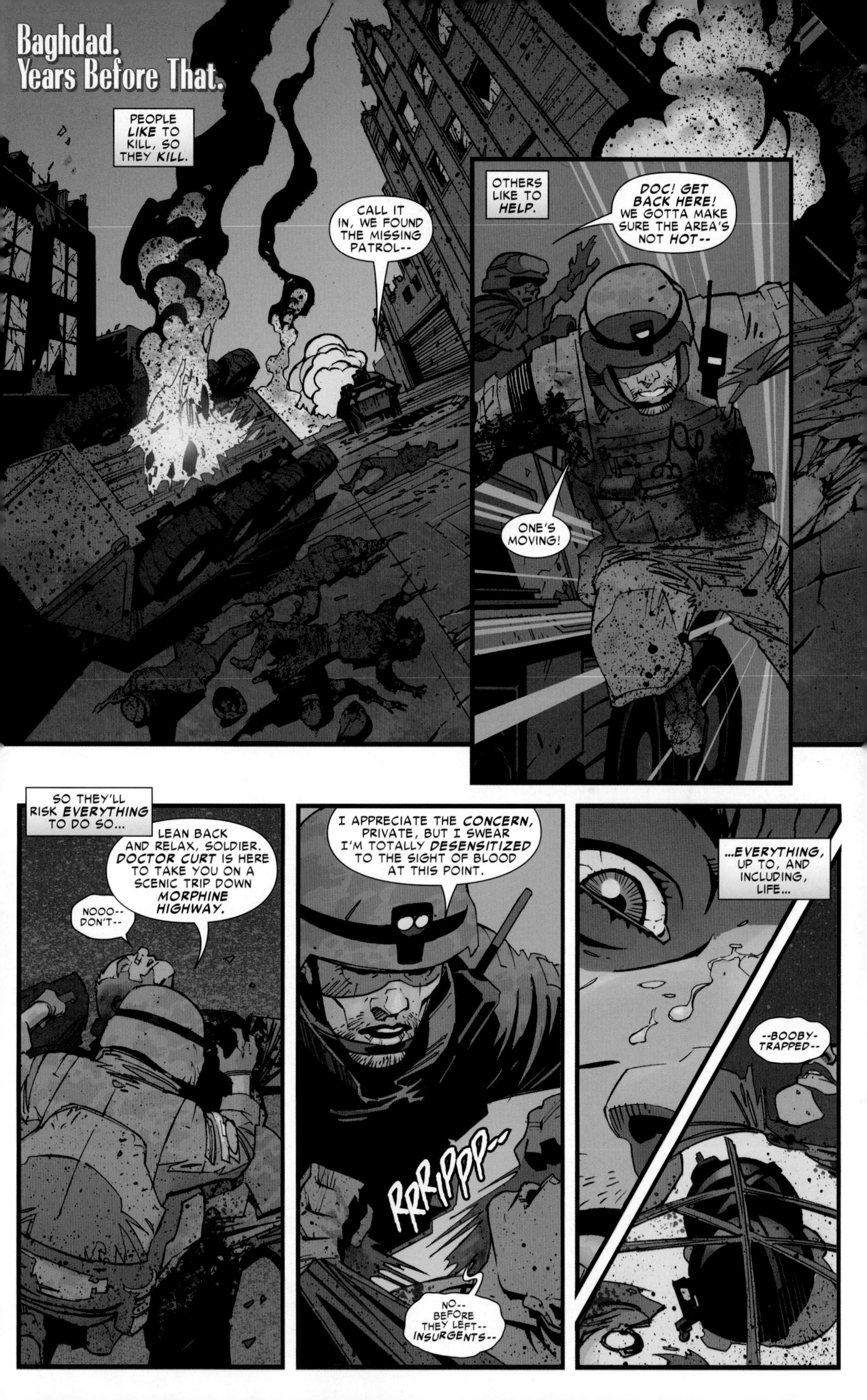
Baghdad.
Years Before That.
PEOPLE LIKE TO KILL, SO THEY KILL.
CALL IT IN, WE FOUND THE MISSING PATROL--
OTHERS LIKE TO HELP.
DOC! GET BACK HERE! WE GOTTA MAKE SURE THE AREA'S NOT HOT--
ONE'S MOVING!
SO THEY'LL RISK EVERYTHING TO DO SO...
LEAN BACK AND RELAX, SOLDIER. DOCTOR CURT IS HERE TO TAKE YOU ON A SCENIC TRIP DOWN MORPHINE HIGHWAY.
NOOO-- DON'T--
I APPRECIATE THE CONCERN, PRIVATE, BUT I SWEAR I'M TOTALLY DESENSITIZED TO THE SIGHT OF BLOOD AT THIS POINT.
RRRIPPP--
NO-- BEFORE THEY LEFT-- INSURGENTS--
...EVERYTHING, UP TO, AND INCLUDING, LIFE...
--BOOBY-TRAPPED--

...AND LIMB.

DASHDGHS
AGDHAGSDHJ
SAHJDGHGAJDG

YJHJIYJLJTHJ
BHGRHJGBW
EF

...THE QUESTION *IS*, REALLY, WHICH IS MORE *COST-EFFECTIVE:*

"TEACHING" MUSCLE AND BONE TO BE AS *"SMART"* AS *SKIN...*

...*OR* IMPLANTING POLYMER FIBERS IN TISSUE TO *GUIDE* CELLS IN REGENERATION POST-INJURY, LIKE AN *AMPHIBIAN* OR A--

NANO-SCAFFOLDING... YOU'RE TALKING ABOUT...

WHOA!

GET A NURSE-- HE'S COMING TO!

YOU'RE IN A CASH®, BROTHER--TAKE IT EASY!

WHERE AM I...?

CONNORS, RIGHT? THE HERO MEDIC? WHERE'D YOU HEAR ABOUT NANO-SCAFFOLDING?

* C.S.H., OR COMBAT SUPPORT HOSPITAL. --GEN. BRENNAN

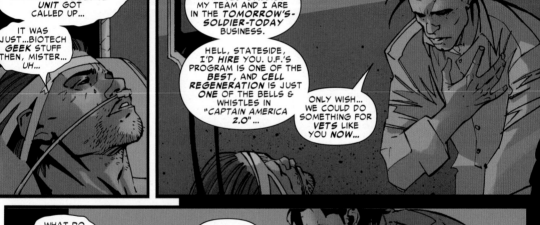

WAS WORKING...FOR MEDICAL RESEARCH AT U.F... UNIVERSITY OF FLORIDA... BEFORE MY RESERVE UNIT GOT CALLED UP...

IT WAS JUST...BIOTECH GEEK STUFF THEN, MISTER... UH...

DOCTOR, SAME AS YOU, PAL. TED SALLIS. MY TEAM AND I ARE IN THE TOMORROW'S-SOLDIER-TODAY BUSINESS.

HELL, STATESIDE, I'D HIRE YOU. U.F.'S PROGRAM IS ONE OF THE BEST, AND CELL REGENERATION IS JUST ONE OF THE BELLS & WHISTLES IN "CAPTAIN AMERICA 2.0"...

ONLY WISH... WE COULD DO SOMETHING FOR VETS LIKE YOU NOW...

WHAT DO YOU MEAN? WHY WOULD I NEED...?

OH...DAMN, I'M SORRY-- I THOUGHT YOU KNEW--

NURSE! I NEED HELP HERE!!

AHHHHH...

AHHHHHHHH!!!

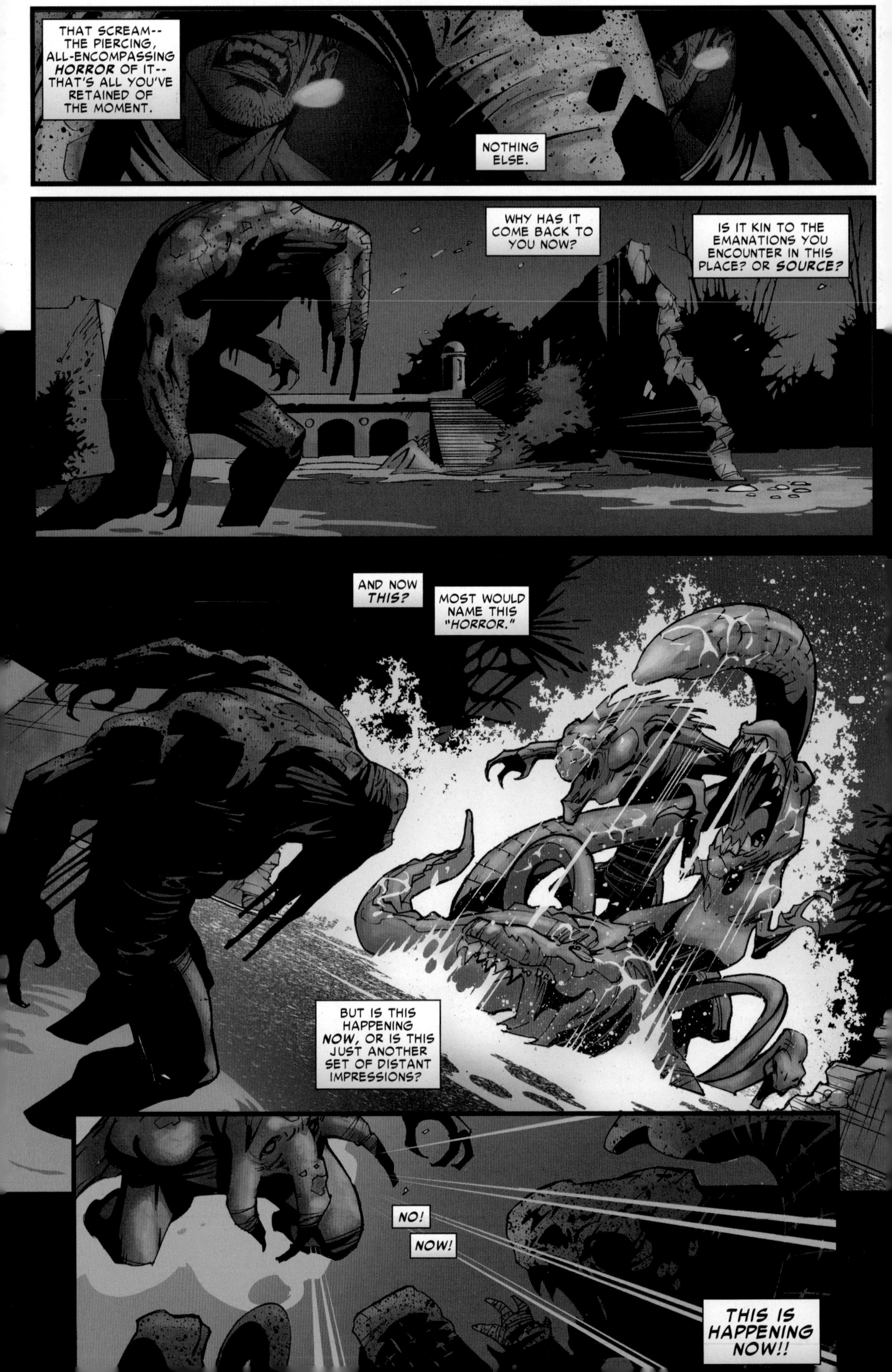
THAT SCREAM-- THE PIERCING, ALL-ENCOMPASSING *HORROR* OF IT-- THAT'S ALL YOU'VE RETAINED OF THE MOMENT.
NOTHING ELSE.
WHY HAS IT COME BACK TO YOU NOW?
IS IT KIN TO THE EMANATIONS YOU ENCOUNTER IN THIS PLACE? OR *SOURCE?*
AND NOW *THIS?*
MOST WOULD NAME THIS "*HORROR.*"
BUT IS THIS HAPPENING *NOW*, OR IS THIS JUST ANOTHER SET OF DISTANT IMPRESSIONS?
NO!
NOW!
THIS IS HAPPENING NOW!!

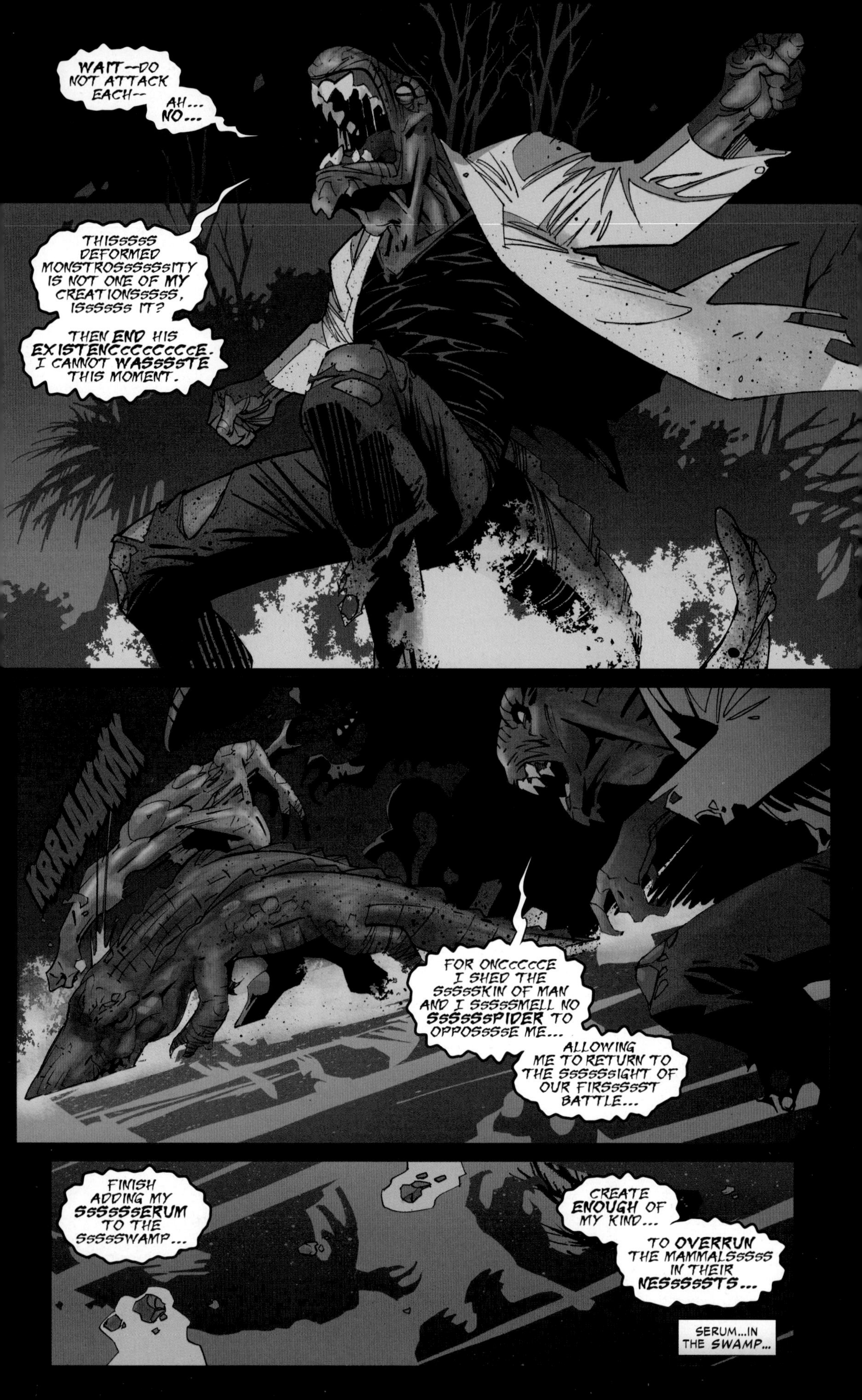
WAIT--DO NOT ATTACK EACH--
AH... NO...
THISSSSS DEFORMED MONSTROSSSSSSITY IS NOT ONE OF MY CREATIONSSSSS, ISSSSSS IT?
THEN END HIS EXISTENCCCCCCCCE. I CANNOT WASSSSTE THIS MOMENT.
KRRAAAKKK
FOR ONCCCCCE I SHED THE SSSSSKIN OF MAN AND I SSSSSMELL NO SSSSSSPIDER TO OPPOSSSSE ME...
ALLOWING ME TO RETURN TO THE SSSSSSIGHT OF OUR FIRSSSSST BATTLE...
FINISH ADDING MY SSSSSSERUM TO THE SSSSSWAMP...
CREATE ENOUGH OF MY KIND...
TO OVERRUN THE MAMMALSSSSS IN THEIR NESSSSSTS...
SERUM...IN THE SWAMP...

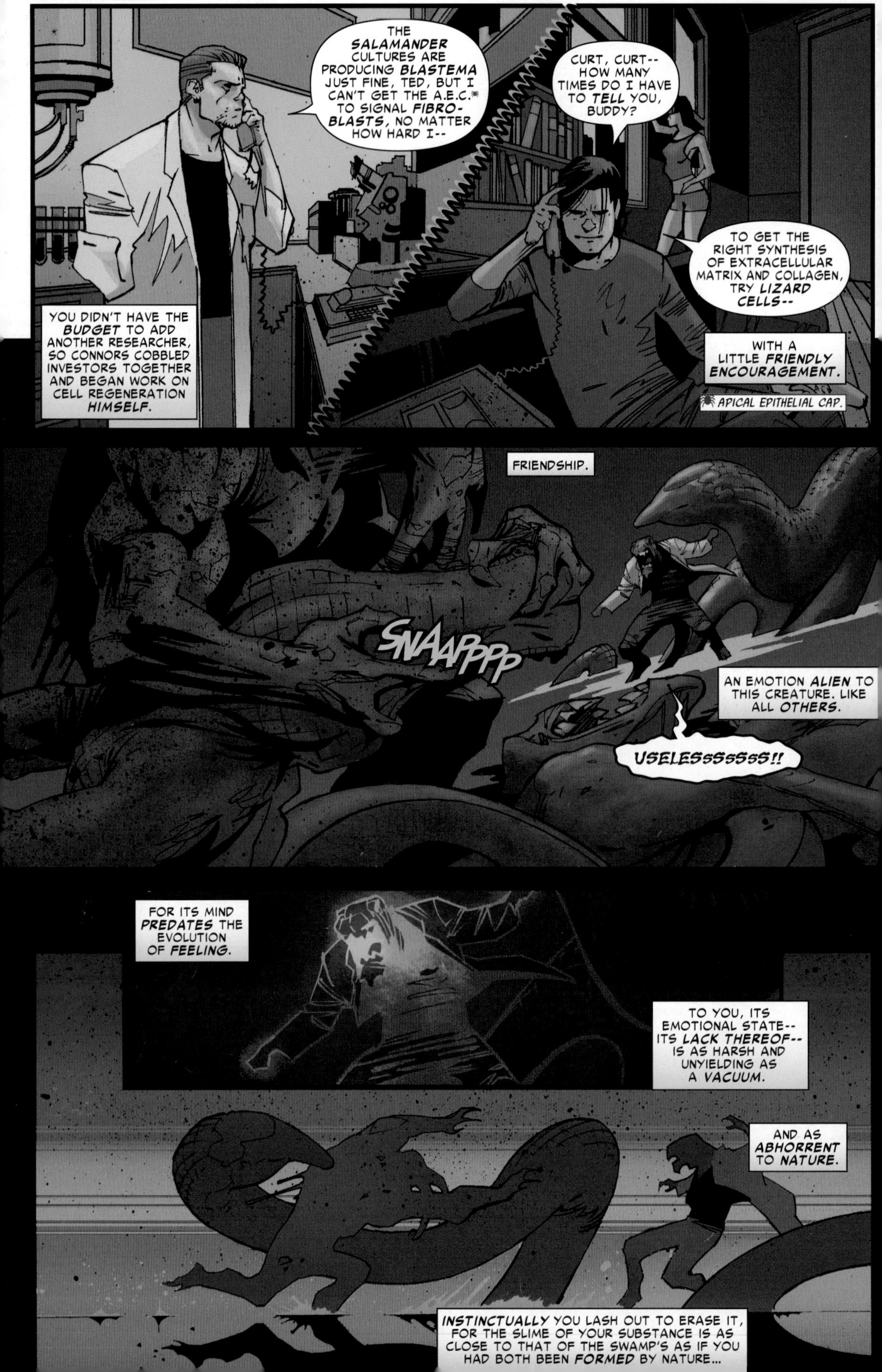
THE SALAMANDER CULTURES ARE PRODUCING BLASTEMA JUST FINE, TED, BUT I CAN'T GET THE A.E.C. TO SIGNAL FIBRO-BLASTS, NO MATTER HOW HARD I--
CURT, CURT-- HOW MANY TIMES DO I HAVE TO TELL YOU, BUDDY?
TO GET THE RIGHT SYNTHESIS OF EXTRACELLULAR MATRIX AND COLLAGEN, TRY LIZARD CELLS--
YOU DIDN'T HAVE THE BUDGET TO ADD ANOTHER RESEARCHER, SO CONNORS COBBLED INVESTORS TOGETHER AND BEGAN WORK ON CELL REGENERATION HIMSELF.
WITH A LITTLE FRIENDLY ENCOURAGEMENT.
APICAL EPITHELIAL CAP.
FRIENDSHIP.
SNAAPPPP
AN EMOTION ALIEN TO THIS CREATURE. LIKE ALL OTHERS.
USELESSSSSSS!!
FOR ITS MIND PREDATES THE EVOLUTION OF FEELING.
TO YOU, ITS EMOTIONAL STATE-- ITS LACK THEREOF-- IS AS HARSH AND UNYIELDING AS A VACUUM.
AND AS ABHORRENT TO NATURE.
INSTINCTUALLY YOU LASH OUT TO ERASE IT, FOR THE SLIME OF YOUR SUBSTANCE IS AS CLOSE TO THAT OF THE SWAMP'S AS IF YOU HAD BOTH BEEN FORMED BY NATURE...

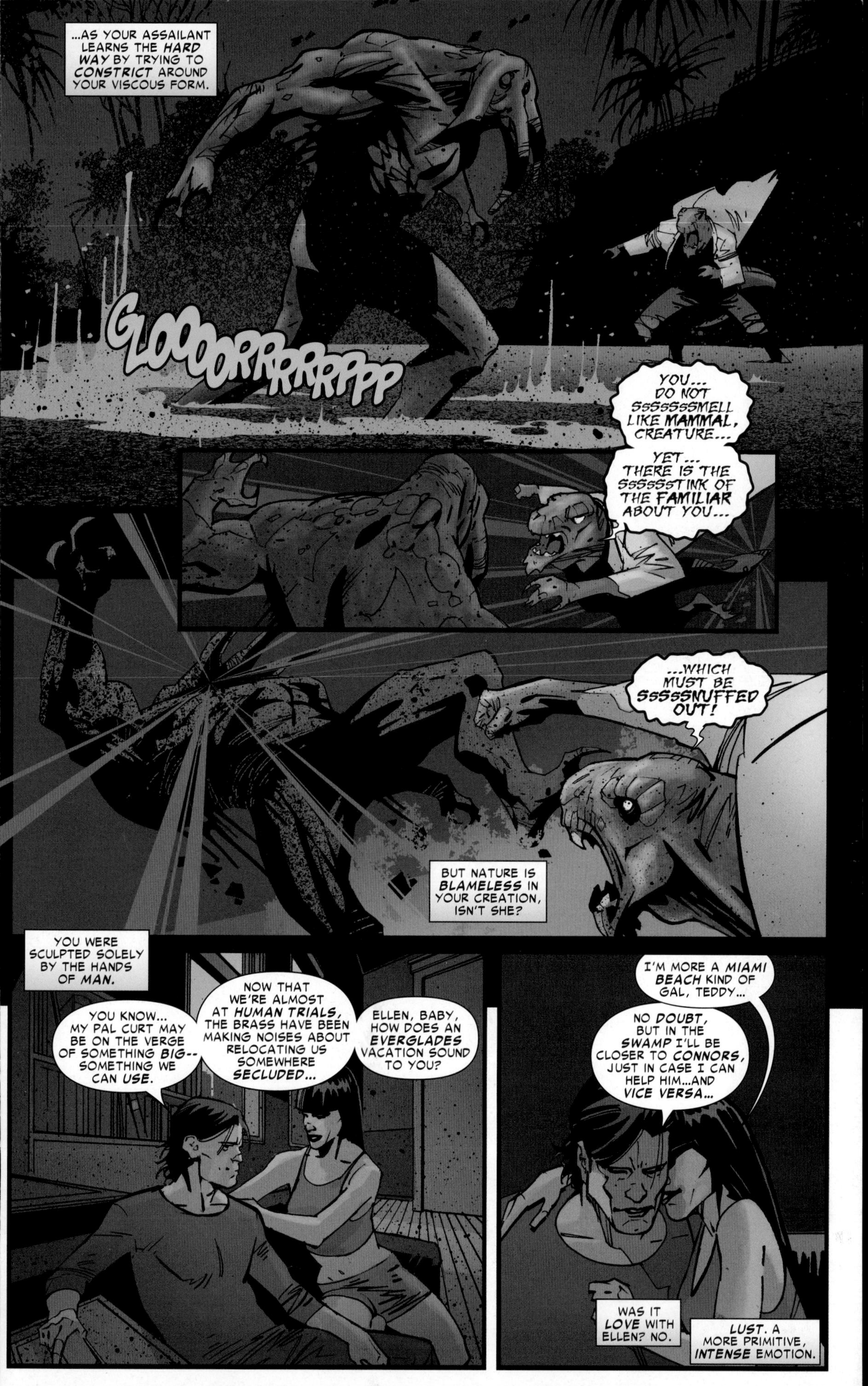
...AS YOUR ASSAILANT LEARNS THE HARD WAY BY TRYING TO CONSTRICT AROUND YOUR VISCOUS FORM.
GLOOOORRRRRRPPP
YOU... DO NOT SSSSSSSMELL LIKE MAMMAL CREATURE...
YET... THERE IS THE SSSSSSTINK OF THE FAMILIAR ABOUT YOU...
...WHICH MUST BE SSSSSNUFFED OUT!
BUT NATURE IS BLAMELESS IN YOUR CREATION, ISN'T SHE?
YOU WERE SCULPTED SOLELY BY THE HANDS OF MAN.
YOU KNOW... MY PAL CURT MAY BE ON THE VERGE OF SOMETHING BIG-- SOMETHING WE CAN USE.
NOW THAT WE'RE ALMOST AT HUMAN TRIALS, THE BRASS HAVE BEEN MAKING NOISES ABOUT RELOCATING US SOMEWHERE SECLUDED...
ELLEN, BABY, HOW DOES AN EVERGLADES VACATION SOUND TO YOU?
I'M MORE A MIAMI BEACH KIND OF GAL, TEDDY...
NO DOUBT, BUT IN THE SWAMP I'LL BE CLOSER TO CONNORS, JUST IN CASE I CAN HELP HIM...AND VICE VERSA...
WAS IT LOVE WITH ELLEN? NO.
LUST. A MORE PRIMITIVE, INTENSE EMOTION.

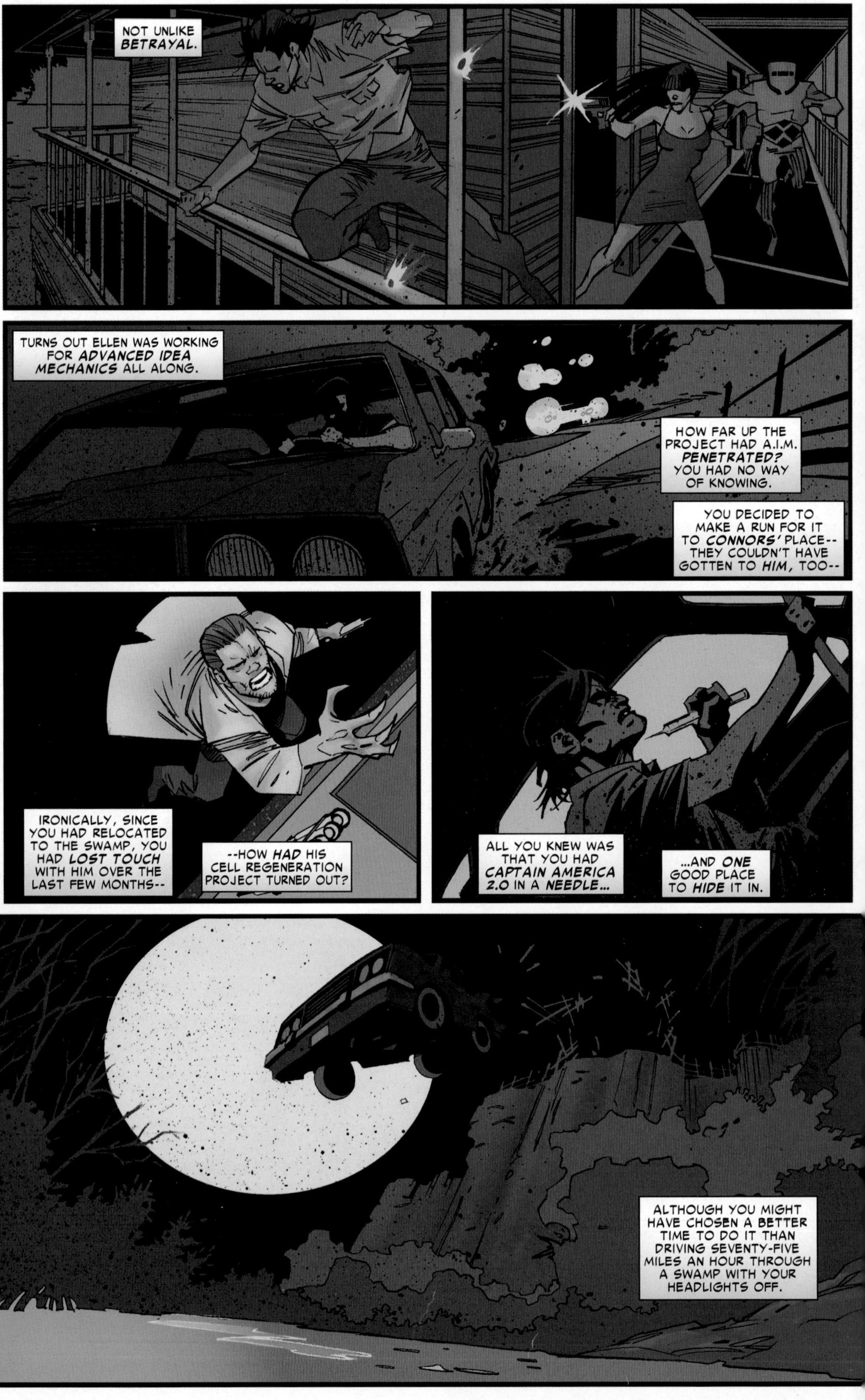
NOT UNLIKE BETRAYAL.
TURNS OUT ELLEN WAS WORKING FOR ADVANCED IDEA MECHANICS ALL ALONG.
HOW FAR UP THE PROJECT HAD A.I.M. PENETRATED? YOU HAD NO WAY OF KNOWING.
YOU DECIDED TO MAKE A RUN FOR IT TO CONNORS' PLACE-- THEY COULDN'T HAVE GOTTEN TO HIM, TOO--
IRONICALLY, SINCE YOU HAD RELOCATED TO THE SWAMP, YOU HAD LOST TOUCH WITH HIM OVER THE LAST FEW MONTHS--
--HOW HAD HIS CELL REGENERATION PROJECT TURNED OUT?
ALL YOU KNEW WAS THAT YOU HAD CAPTAIN AMERICA 2.0 IN A NEEDLE...
...AND ONE GOOD PLACE TO HIDE IT IN.
ALTHOUGH YOU MIGHT HAVE CHOSEN A BETTER TIME TO DO IT THAN DRIVING SEVENTY-FIVE MILES AN HOUR THROUGH A SWAMP WITH YOUR HEADLIGHTS OFF.

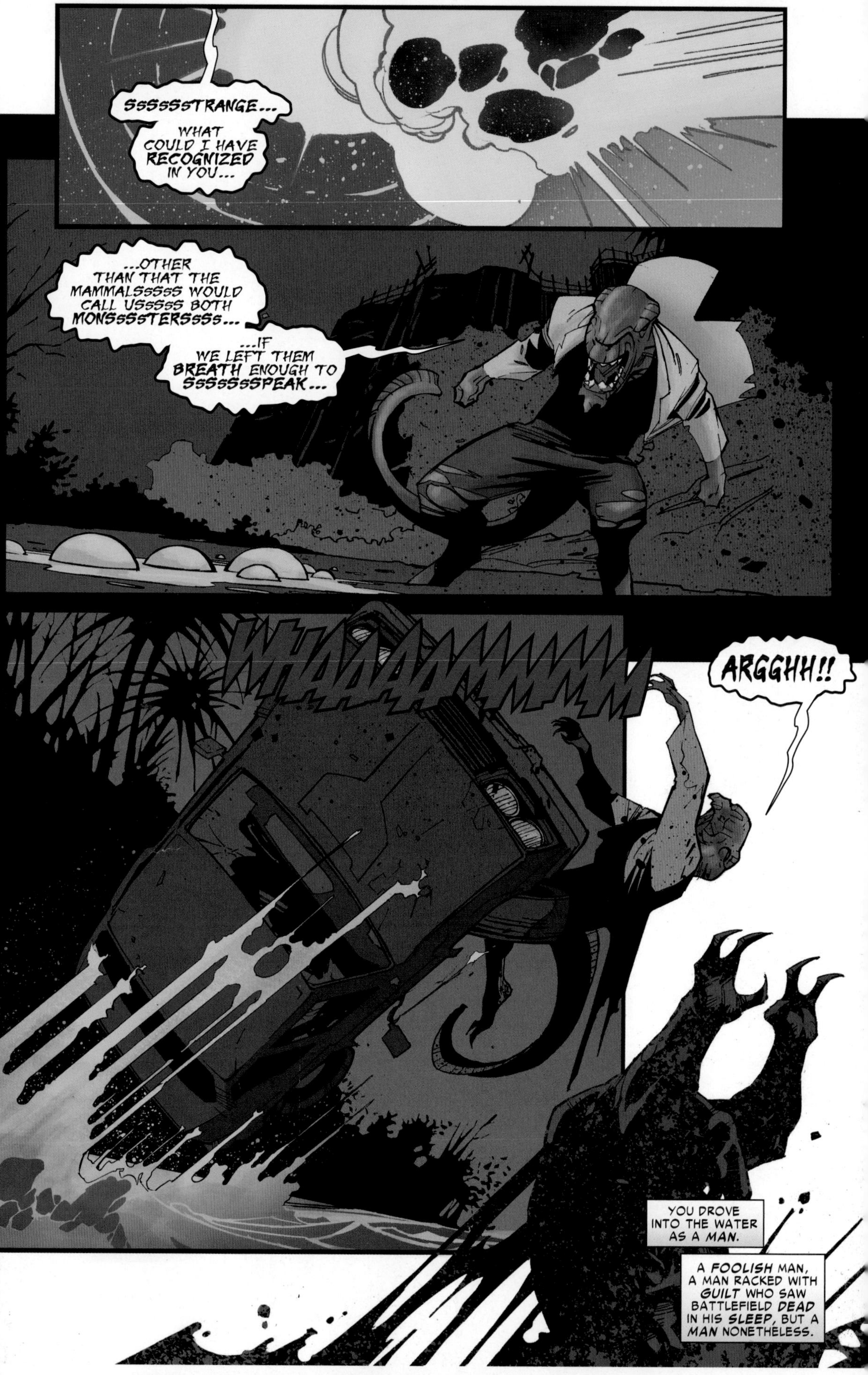
SSSSSSTRANGE...
WHAT COULD I HAVE RECOGNIZED IN YOU...
...OTHER THAN THAT THE MAMMALSSSSS WOULD CALL USSSSS BOTH MONSSSSTERSSSS...
...IF WE LEFT THEM BREATH ENOUGH TO SSSSSSSPEAK...
WHAAAMMMM
ARGGHH!!
YOU DROVE INTO THE WATER AS A MAN.
A FOOLISH MAN, A MAN RACKED WITH GUILT WHO SAW BATTLEFIELD DEAD IN HIS SLEEP, BUT A MAN NONETHELESS.

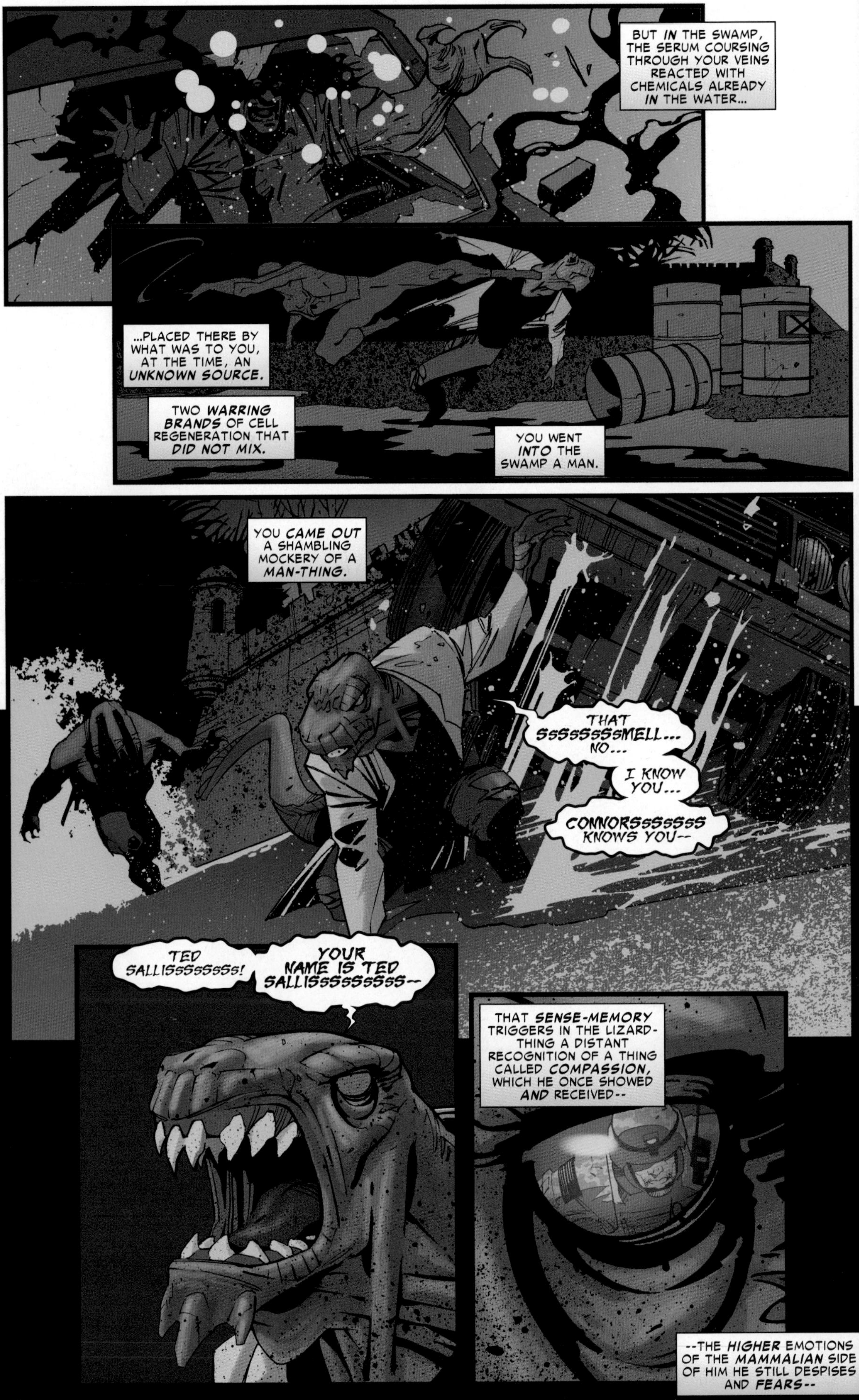
BUT IN THE SWAMP, THE SERUM COURSING THROUGH YOUR VEINS REACTED WITH CHEMICALS ALREADY IN THE WATER...
...PLACED THERE BY WHAT WAS TO YOU, AT THE TIME, AN UNKNOWN SOURCE.
TWO WARRING BRANDS OF CELL REGENERATION THAT DID NOT MIX.
YOU WENT INTO THE SWAMP A MAN.
YOU CAME OUT A SHAMBLING MOCKERY OF A MAN-THING.
THAT SSSSSSSSMELL... NO...
I KNOW YOU...
CONNORSSSSSSS KNOWS YOU--
TED SALLISSSSSSSS!
YOUR NAME IS TED SALLISSSSSSSSS--
THAT SENSE-MEMORY TRIGGERS IN THE LIZARD-THING A DISTANT RECOGNITION OF A THING CALLED COMPASSION, WHICH HE ONCE SHOWED AND RECEIVED--
--THE HIGHER EMOTIONS OF THE MAMMALIAN SIDE OF HIM HE STILL DESPISES AND FEARS--

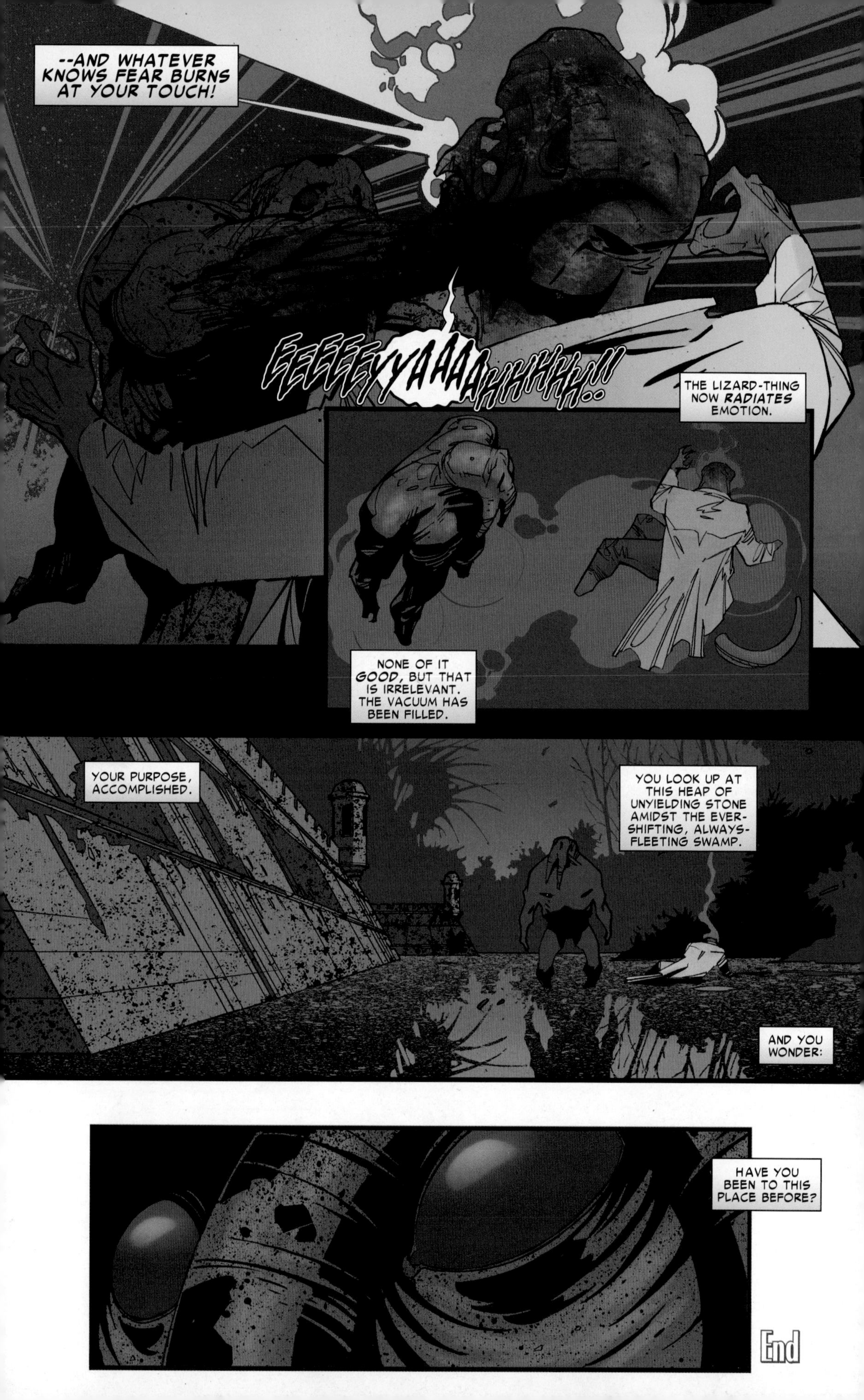
--AND WHATEVER KNOWS FEAR BURNS AT YOUR TOUCH!
EEEEEEYYAAAAHHHHH!!
THE LIZARD-THING NOW RADIATES EMOTION.
NONE OF IT GOOD, BUT THAT IS IRRELEVANT. THE VACUUM HAS BEEN FILLED.
YOUR PURPOSE, ACCOMPLISHED.
YOU LOOK UP AT THIS HEAP OF UNYIELDING STONE AMIDST THE EVER-SHIFTING, ALWAYS-FLEETING SWAMP.
AND YOU WONDER:
HAVE YOU BEEN TO THIS PLACE BEFORE?
End

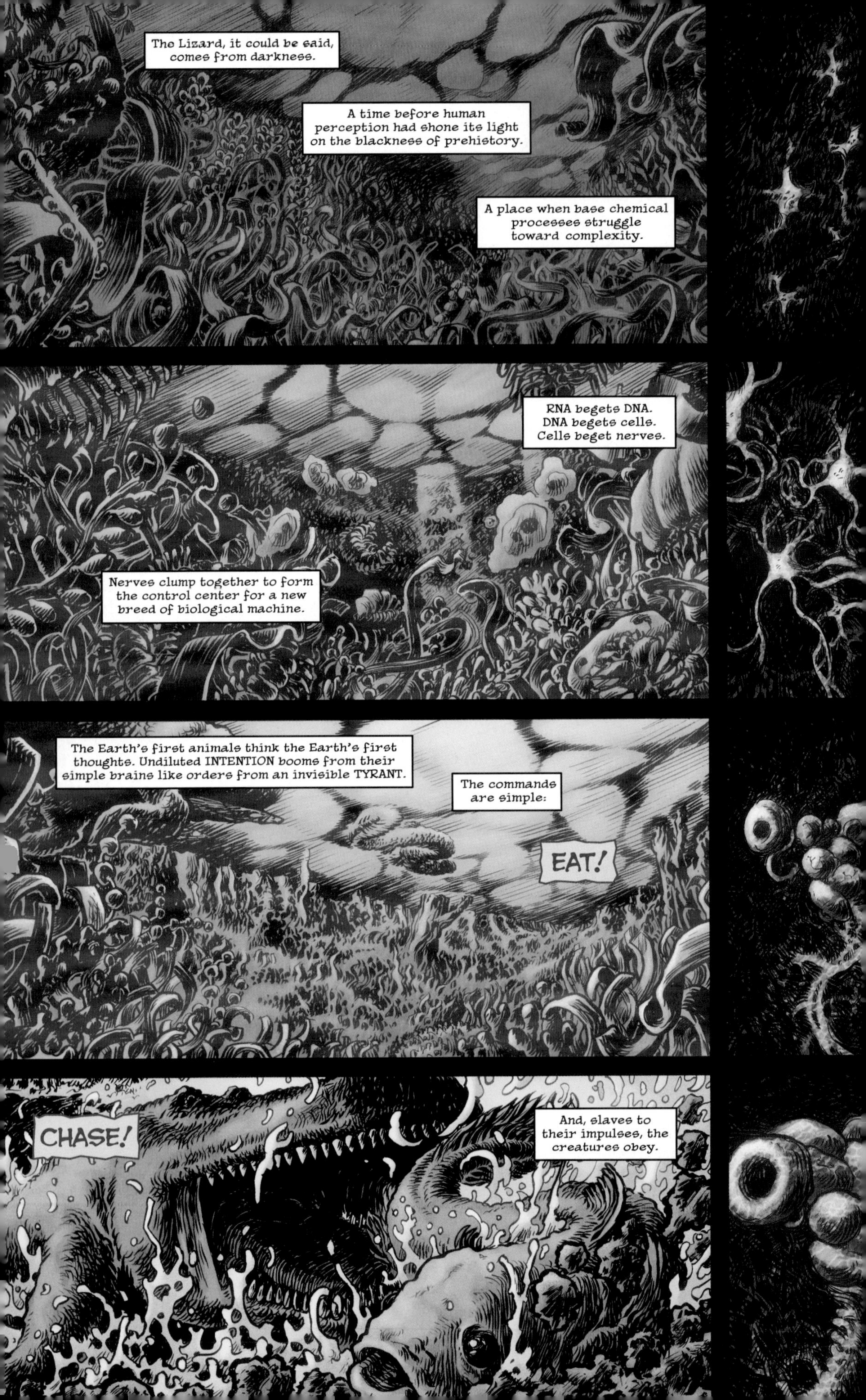
The Lizard, it could be said, comes from darkness.
A time before human perception had shone its light on the blackness of prehistory.
A place when base chemical processes struggle toward complexity.
RNA begets DNA. DNA begets cells. Cells beget nerves.
Nerves clump together to form the control center for a new breed of biological machine.
The Earth's first animals think the Earth's first thoughts. Undiluted INTENTION booms from their simple brains like orders from an invisible TYRANT.
The commands are simple:
EAT!
CHASE!
And, slaves to their impulses, the creatures obey.

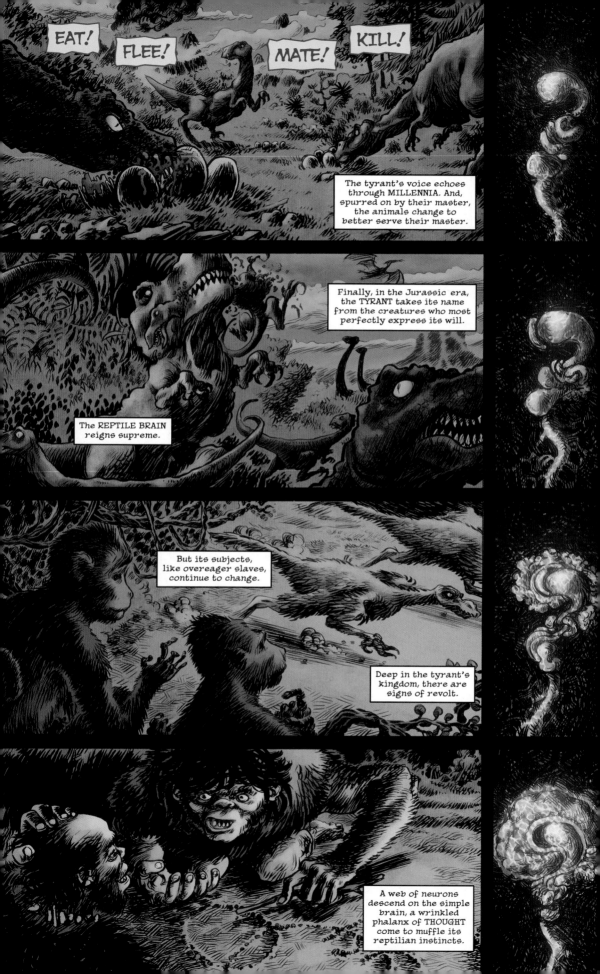

EAT!

FLEE!

MATE!

KILL!

The tyrant's voice echoes through MILLENNIA. And, spurred on by their master, the animals change to better serve their master.

Finally, in the Jurassic era, the TYRANT takes its name from the creatures who most perfectly express its will.

The REPTILE BRAIN reigns supreme.

But its subjects, like overeager slaves, continue to change.

Deep in the tyrant's kingdom, there are signs of revolt.

A web of neurons descend on the simple brain, a wrinkled phalanx of THOUGHT come to muffle its reptilian instincts.

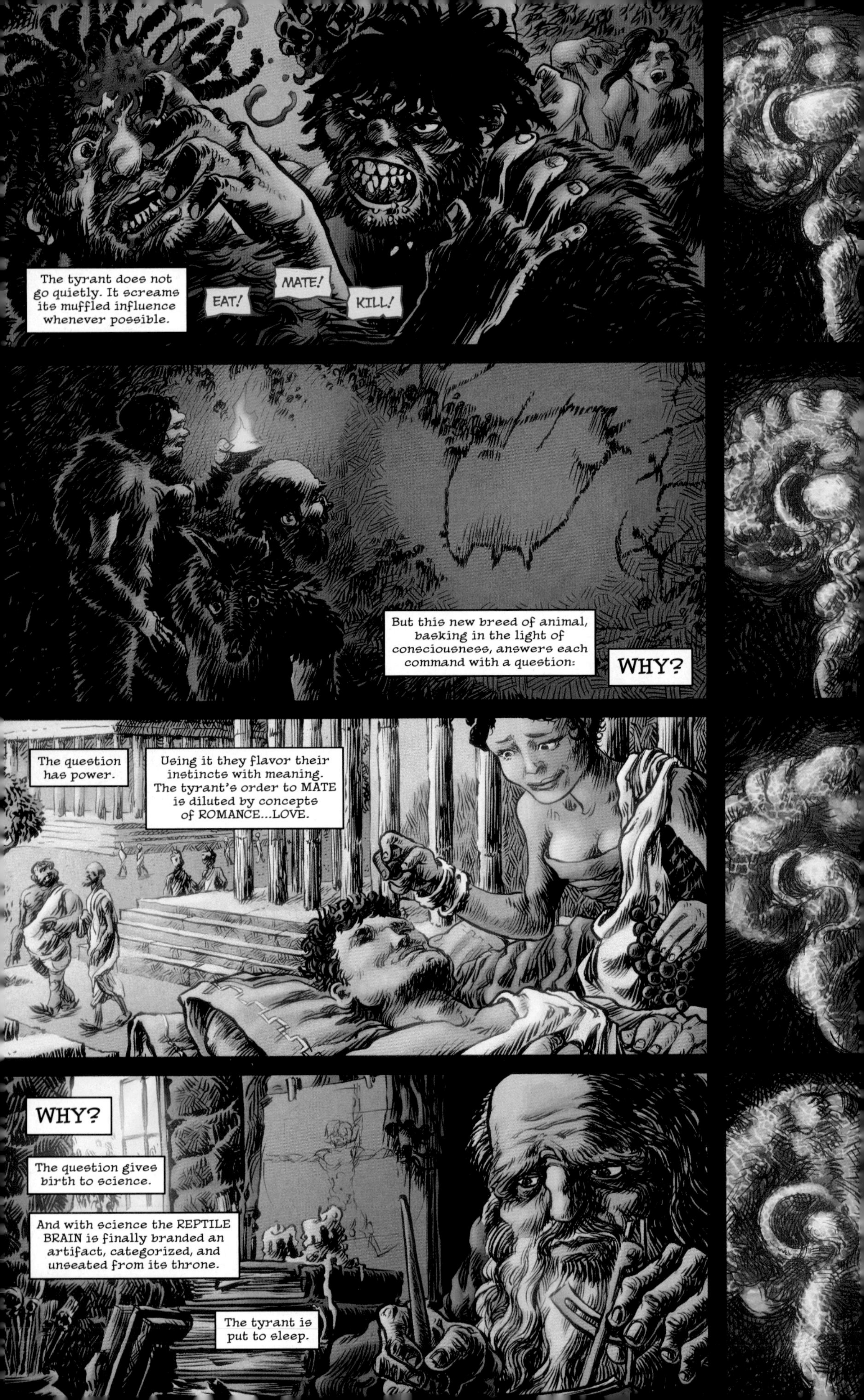
The tyrant does not go quietly. It screams its muffled influence whenever possible.
EAT!
MATE!
KILL!
But this new breed of animal, basking in the light of consciousness, answers each command with a question:
WHY?
The question has power.
Using it they flavor their instincts with meaning. The tyrant's order to MATE is diluted by concepts of ROMANCE...LOVE.
WHY?
The question gives birth to science.
And with science the REPTILE BRAIN is finally branded an artifact, categorized, and unseated from its throne.
The tyrant is put to sleep.

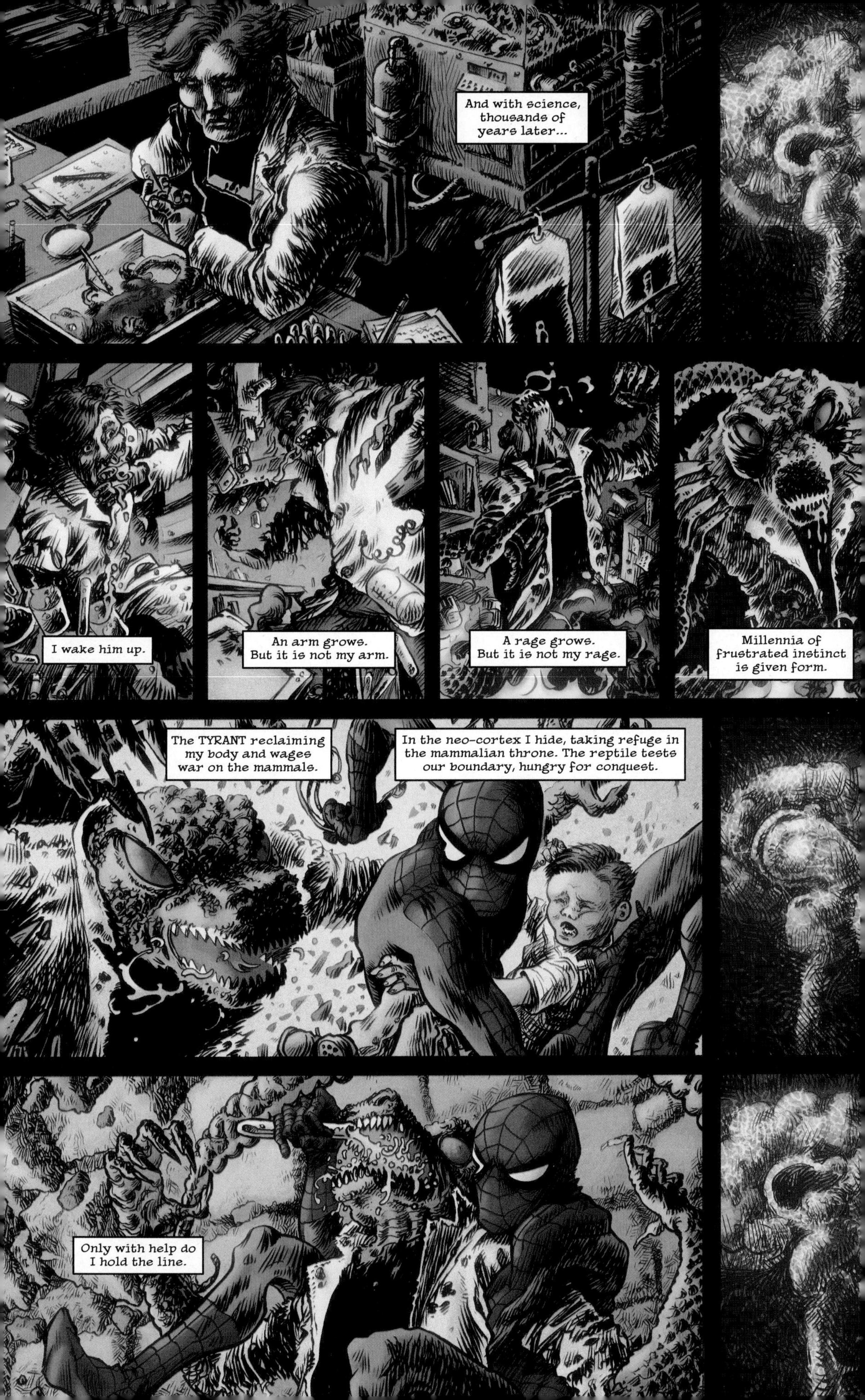
And with science, thousands of years later...
I wake him up.
An arm grows. But it is not my arm.
A rage grows. But it is not my rage.
Millennia of frustrated instinct is given form.
The TYRANT reclaiming my body and wages war on the mammals.
In the neo-cortex I hide, taking refuge in the mammalian throne. The reptile tests our boundary, hungry for conquest.
Only with help do I hold the line.

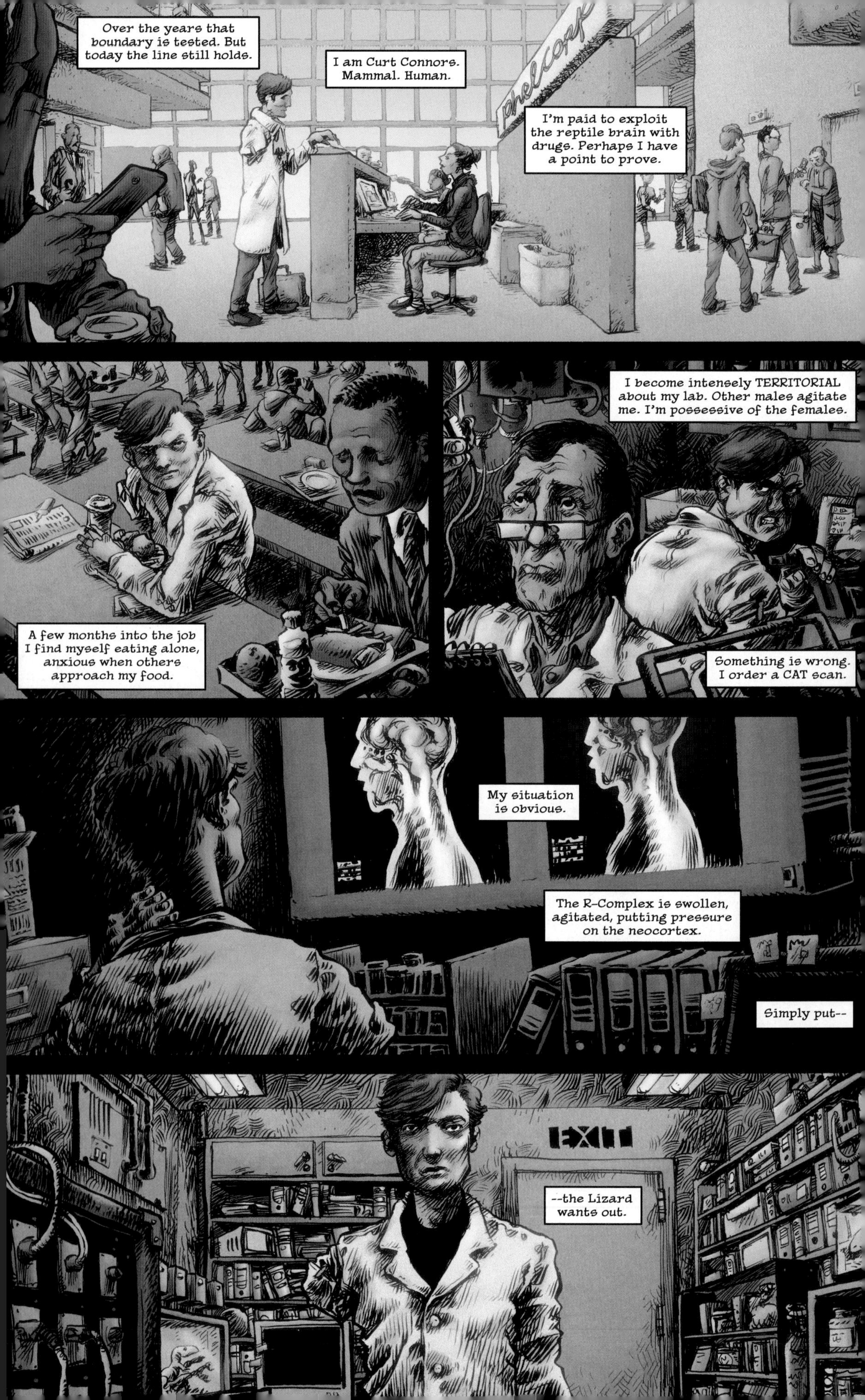

Over the years that boundary is tested. But today the line still holds.
I am Curt Connors. Mammal. Human.
I'm paid to exploit the reptile brain with drugs. Perhaps I have a point to prove.
A few months into the job I find myself eating alone, anxious when others approach my food.
I become intensely TERRITORIAL about my lab. Other males agitate me. I'm possessive of the females.
Something is wrong. I order a CAT scan.
My situation is obvious.
The R-Complex is swollen, agitated, putting pressure on the neocortex.
Simply put--
--the Lizard wants out.

SHED
PRELUDE

ZEB WELLS WRITER · XURXO PENALTA ARTIST

MATT HOLLINGSWORTH COLOR ART · JARED K. FLETCHER LETTERS

TOM BRENNAN ASST. EDITOR · STEPHEN WACKER EDITOR

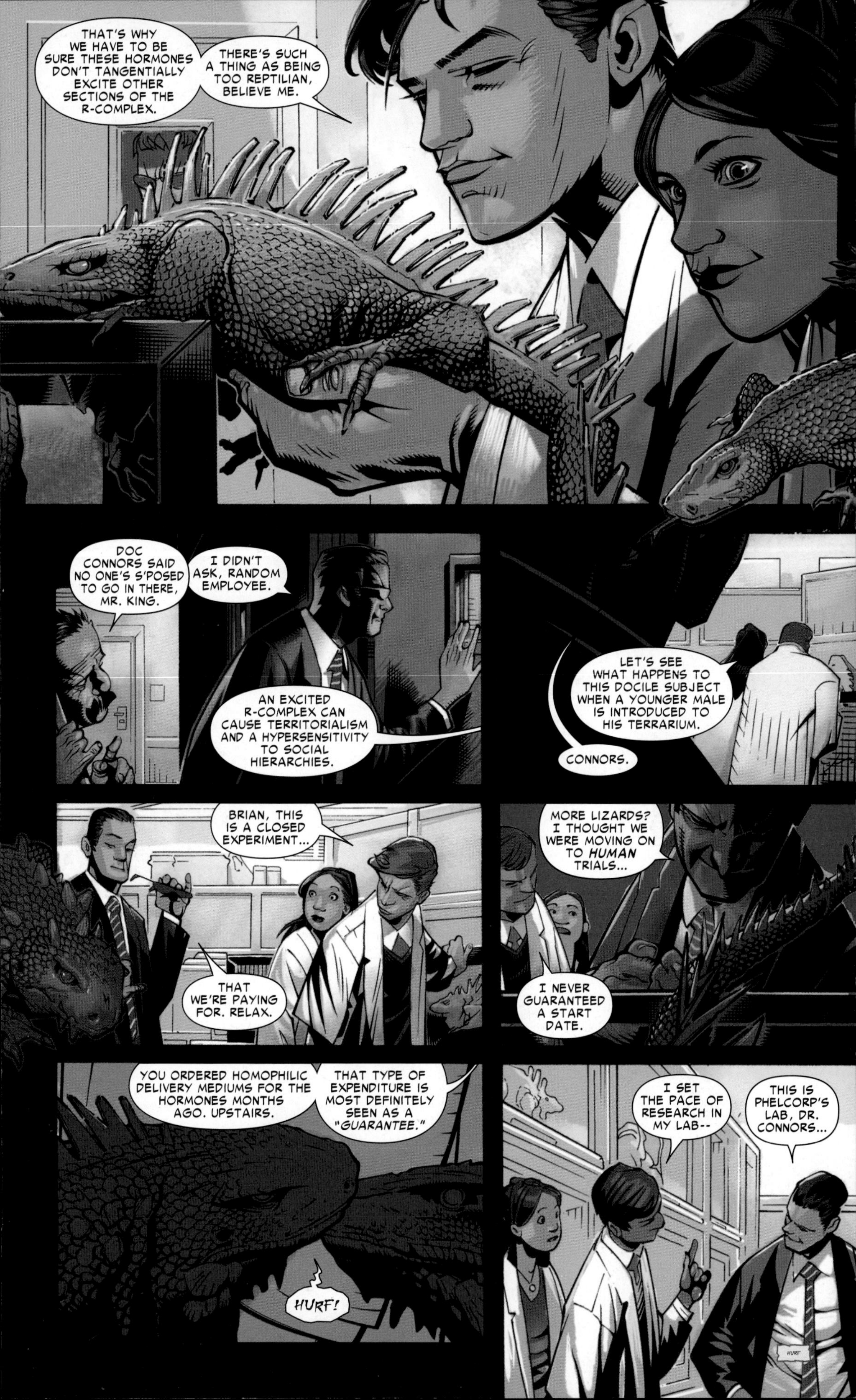
THAT'S WHY WE HAVE TO BE SURE THESE HORMONES DON'T TANGENTIALLY EXCITE OTHER SECTIONS OF THE R-COMPLEX.
THERE'S SUCH A THING AS BEING TOO REPTILIAN, BELIEVE ME.
DOC CONNORS SAID NO ONE'S S'POSED TO GO IN THERE, MR. KING.
I DIDN'T ASK, RANDOM EMPLOYEE.
AN EXCITED R-COMPLEX CAN CAUSE TERRITORIALISM AND A HYPERSENSITIVITY TO SOCIAL HIERARCHIES.
LET'S SEE WHAT HAPPENS TO THIS DOCILE SUBJECT WHEN A YOUNGER MALE IS INTRODUCED TO HIS TERRARIUM.
CONNORS.
BRIAN, THIS IS A CLOSED EXPERIMENT...
THAT WE'RE PAYING FOR. RELAX.
MORE LIZARDS? I THOUGHT WE WERE MOVING ON TO *HUMAN* TRIALS...
I NEVER GUARANTEED A START DATE.
YOU ORDERED HOMOPHILIC DELIVERY MEDIUMS FOR THE HORMONES MONTHS AGO. UPSTAIRS.
THAT TYPE OF EXPENDITURE IS MOST DEFINITELY SEEN AS A "*GUARANTEE.*"
HURF!
I SET THE PACE OF RESEARCH IN MY LAB--
THIS IS PHELCORP'S LAB, DR. CONNORS...
HURF

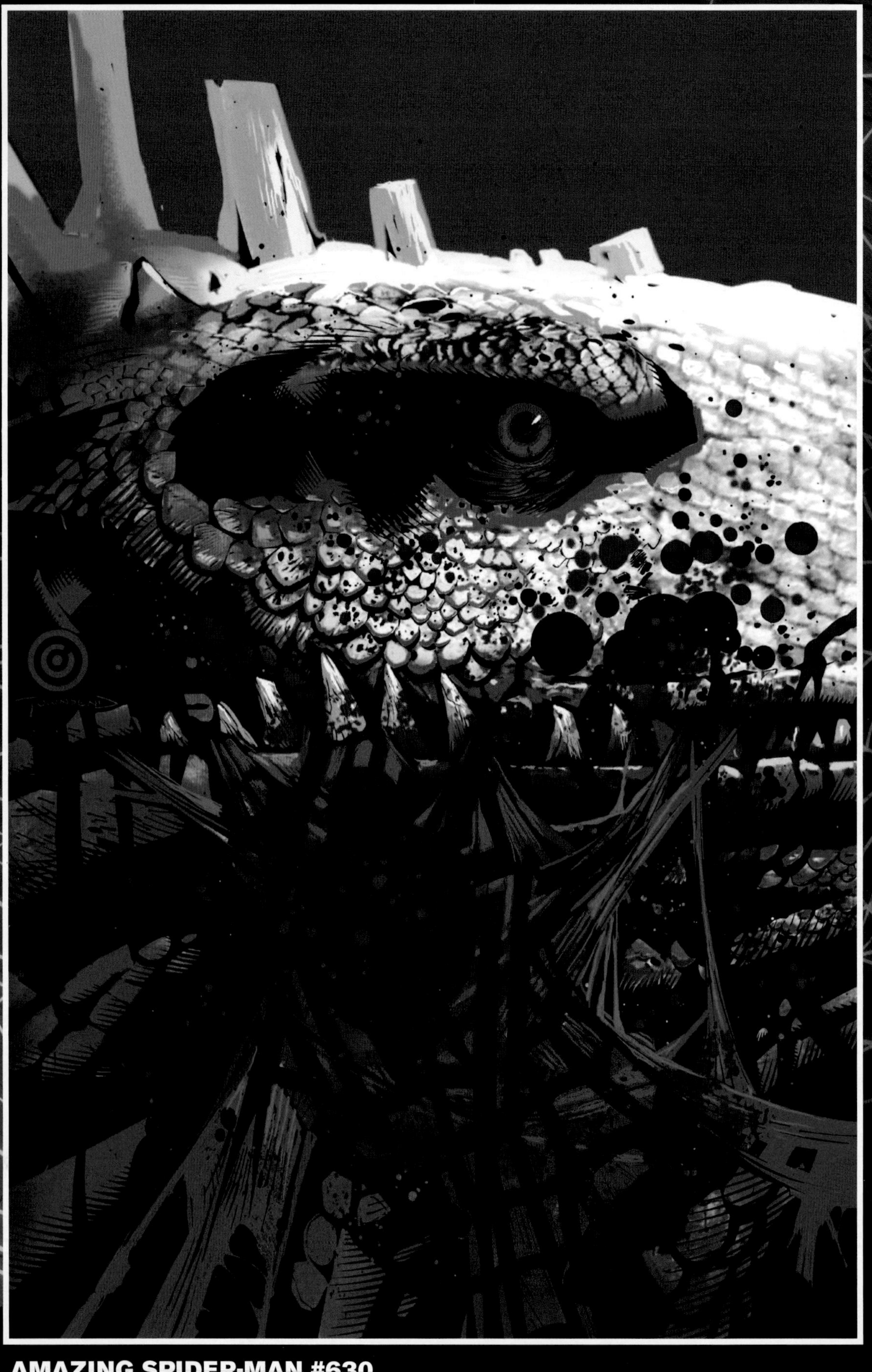

AMAZING SPIDER-MAN #630
COVER BY CHRIS BACHALO & TIM TOWNSEND

INNOVATIONS AT PHELCORP – Phelcorp executive Brian King continues to impress stockholders. His decisions have led to an increase in the company's scientific research departments. Under King's guidance, Phelcorp executives authorized the implementation of a new program studying lizards. more…

IS HOPE LOST? – It is with a heavy heart that Bugle Girl by Betty Brant reports that the NYPD has given up on the rescue efforts in the search for Mattie Franklin and Cassandra Webb. They are now pursuing a "search and recovery" operation. more…

AUNT MAY – ANTI-MAY? – May Parker, local hero and beloved staple of Martin Li's F.E.A.S.T. center, has come under fire from F.E.A.S.T. regulars for "abusive language and behavior"… more…

After a wartime injury, Dr. Curt Connors, once a talented and gifted surgeon, had to endure the amputation of his right arm. Devoting himself to the study of reptilian DNA, Connors attempted to create a serum that would grant his body the power to regenerate lost limbs. The result was an effect the scientist had not foreseen, as he was transformed into a reptilian-humanoid monster known as THE LIZARD. Peter Parker, the Amazing Spider-Man, intervened, stopping the creature and restoring Connors to his normal self.

Things just don't seem to be going well for Peter Parker now, though. After facing down foe after foe, Spider-Man has been drained emotionally and physically. Doctor Octopus, Electro, Mysterio, and even the Rhino have all resurfaced, challenging the web-slinger at every chance they get. Are these bouts with old enemies coincidence, or is someone orchestrating Spidey's terrible luck from behind the scenes?

Adding insult to (serious) injury, Peter's life outside of his costume is proving to be difficult, as well. His uncertainties about dating Carlie Cooper of the NYPD and a casual romance with Felicia Hardy, the BLACK CAT, are only making his personal life even more complicated.

Dealing with unemployment, an aunt who has her hands full with a new marriage, and his own exhaustion, Peter Parker has slowly started to lose steam.

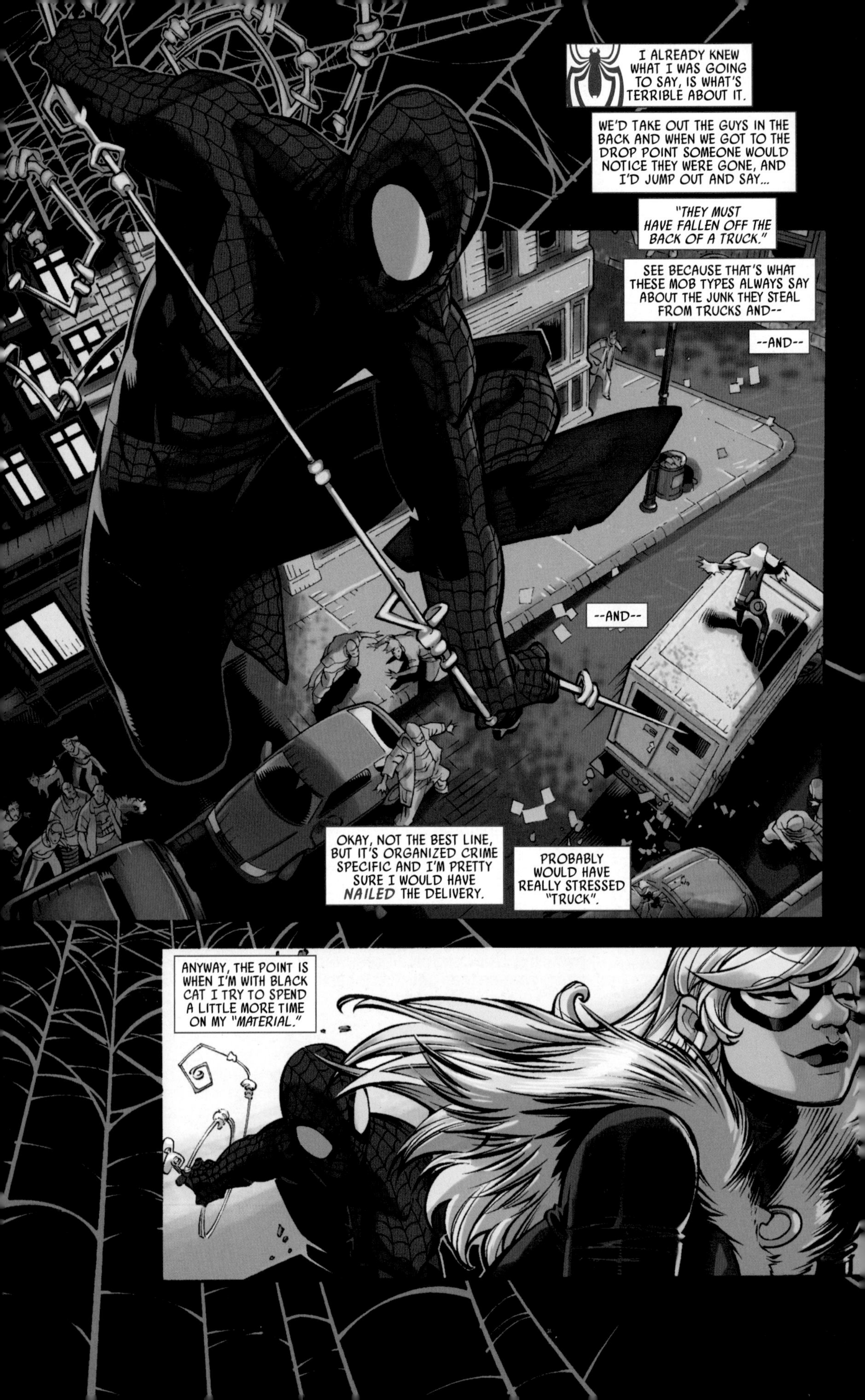
I ALREADY KNEW WHAT I WAS GOING TO SAY, IS WHAT'S TERRIBLE ABOUT IT.
WE'D TAKE OUT THE GUYS IN THE BACK AND WHEN WE GOT TO THE DROP POINT SOMEONE WOULD NOTICE THEY WERE GONE, AND I'D JUMP OUT AND SAY...
"THEY MUST HAVE FALLEN OFF THE BACK OF A TRUCK."
SEE BECAUSE THAT'S WHAT THESE MOB TYPES ALWAYS SAY ABOUT THE JUNK THEY STEAL FROM TRUCKS AND--
--AND--
--AND--
OKAY, NOT THE BEST LINE, BUT IT'S ORGANIZED CRIME SPECIFIC AND I'M PRETTY SURE I WOULD HAVE NAILED THE DELIVERY.
PROBABLY WOULD HAVE REALLY STRESSED "TRUCK".
ANYWAY, THE POINT IS WHEN I'M WITH BLACK CAT I TRY TO SPEND A LITTLE MORE TIME ON MY "MATERIAL."

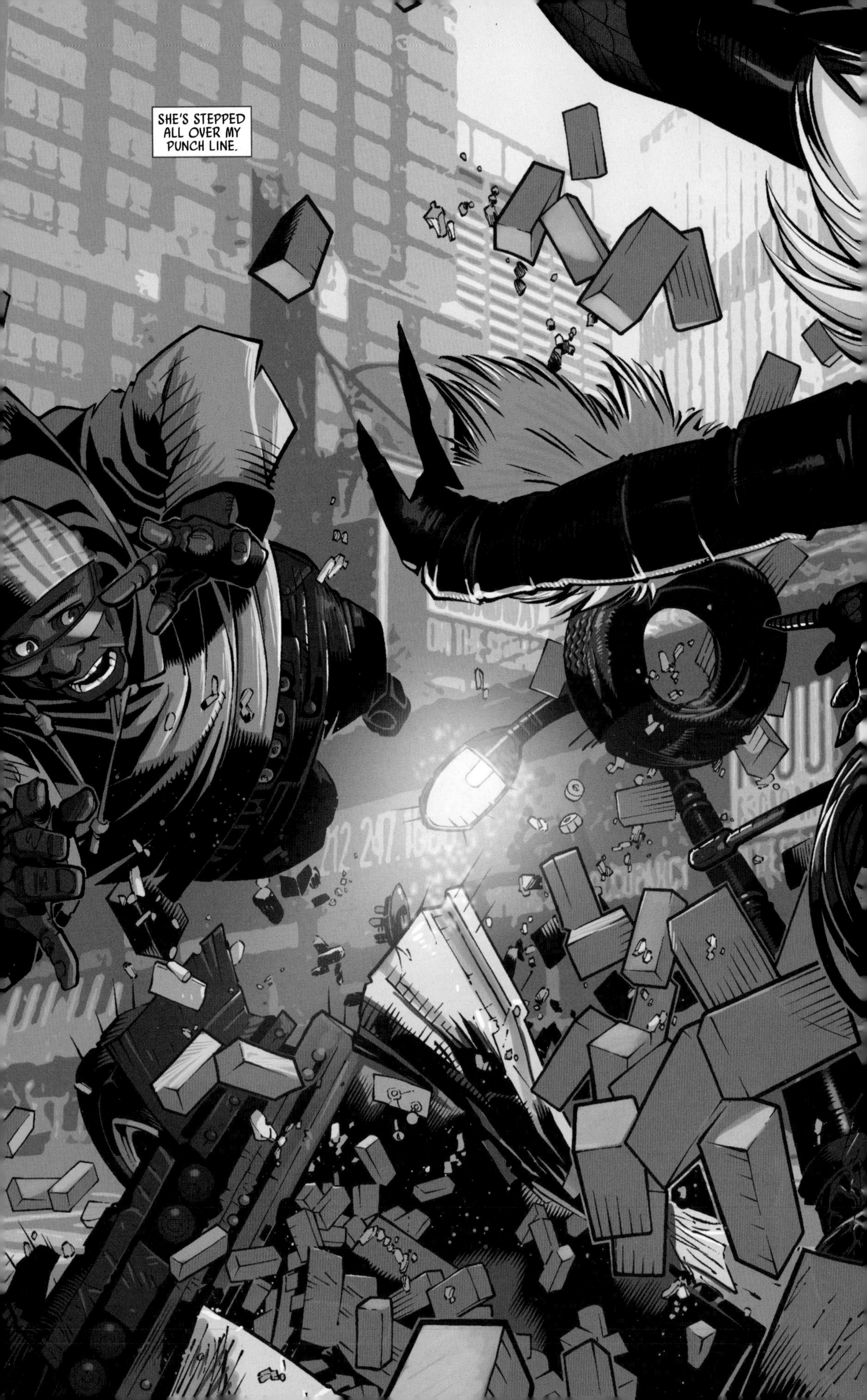
SHE'S STEPPED ALL OVER MY PUNCH LINE.

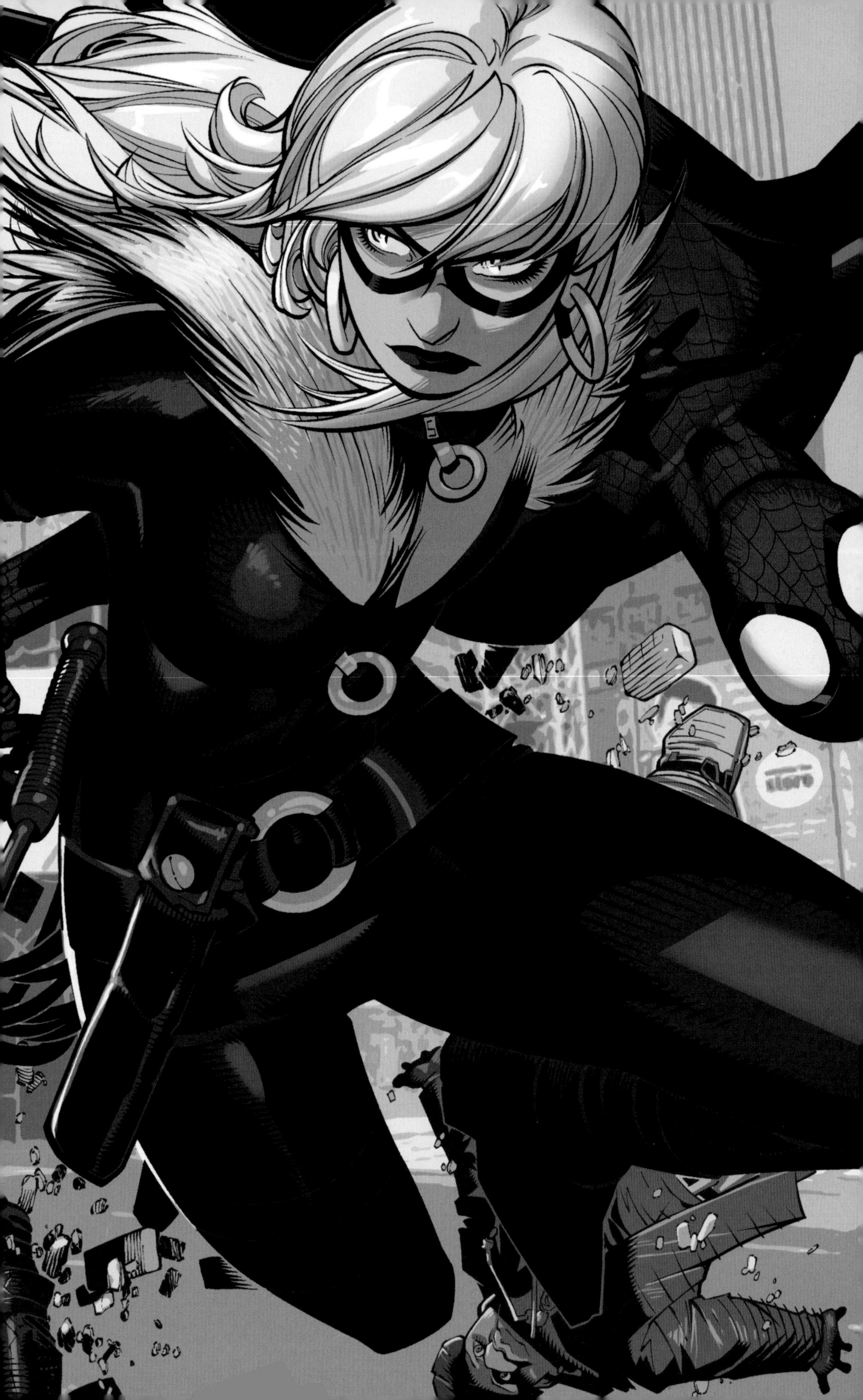

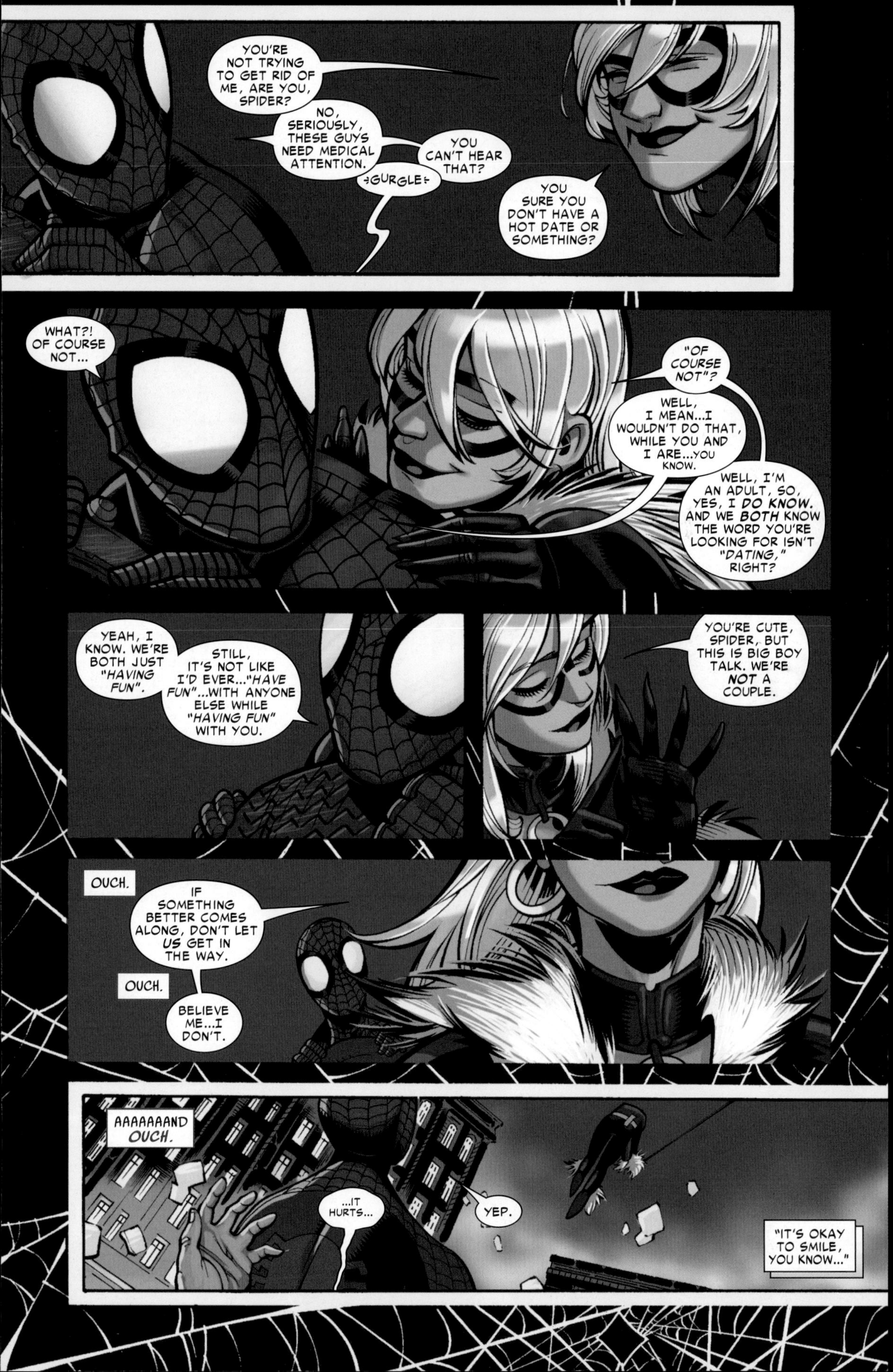
YOU'RE NOT TRYING TO GET RID OF ME, ARE YOU, SPIDER?
NO, SERIOUSLY, THESE GUYS NEED MEDICAL ATTENTION.
YOU CAN'T HEAR THAT?
GURGLE
YOU SURE YOU DON'T HAVE A HOT DATE OR SOMETHING?
WHAT?! OF COURSE NOT...
"OF COURSE NOT"?
WELL, I MEAN...I WOULDN'T DO THAT, WHILE YOU AND I ARE...YOU KNOW.
WELL, I'M AN ADULT, SO, YES, I DO KNOW. AND WE BOTH KNOW THE WORD YOU'RE LOOKING FOR ISN'T "DATING," RIGHT?
YEAH, I KNOW. WE'RE BOTH JUST "HAVING FUN".
STILL, IT'S NOT LIKE I'D EVER..."HAVE FUN"...WITH ANYONE ELSE WHILE "HAVING FUN" WITH YOU.
YOU'RE CUTE, SPIDER, BUT THIS IS BIG BOY TALK. WE'RE NOT A COUPLE.
OUCH.
IF SOMETHING BETTER COMES ALONG, DON'T LET US GET IN THE WAY.
OUCH.
BELIEVE ME...I DON'T.
AAAAAAAND OUCH.
...IT HURTS...
YEP.
"IT'S OKAY TO SMILE, YOU KNOW..."

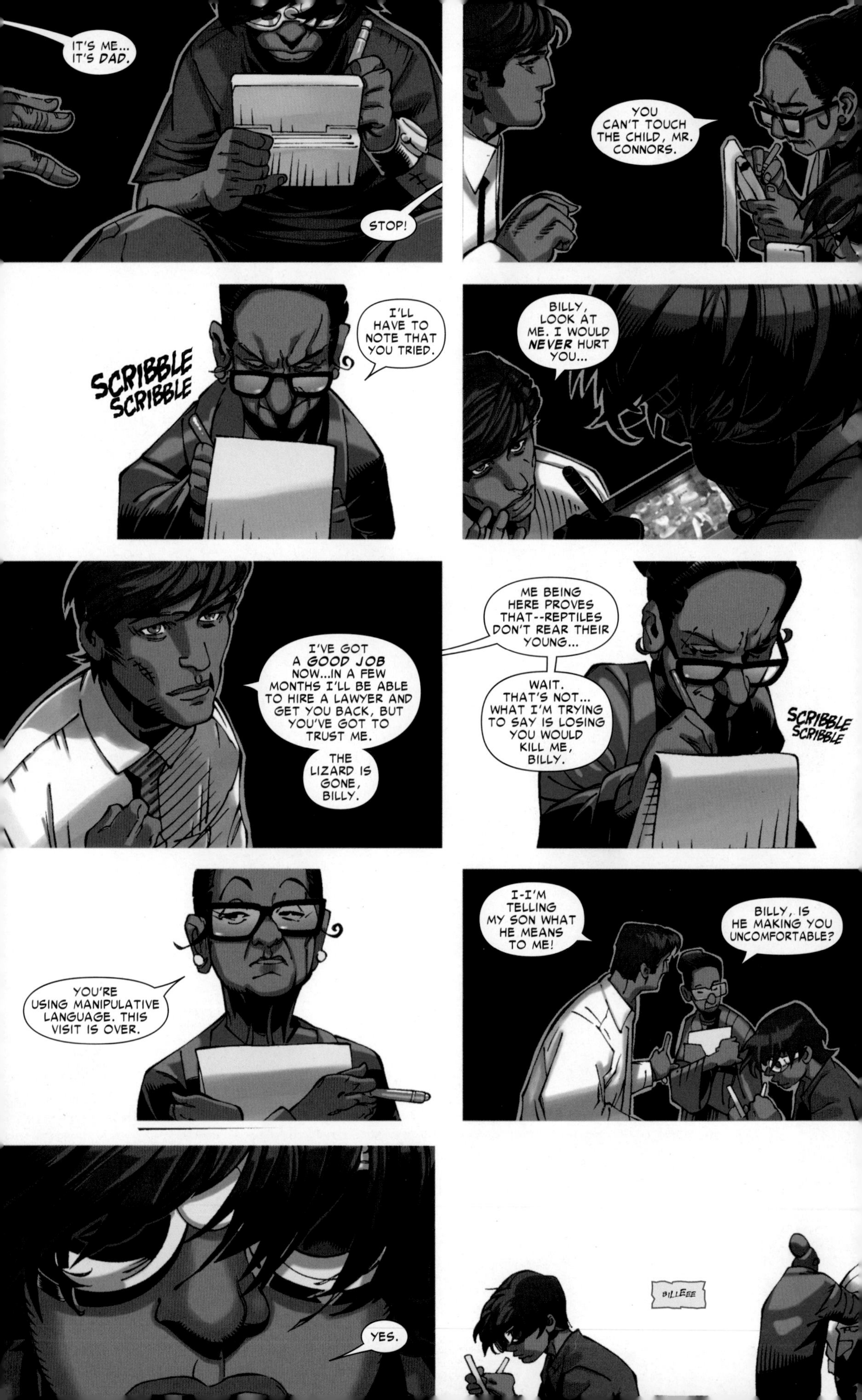
IT'S ME... IT'S DAD.
STOP!
YOU CAN'T TOUCH THE CHILD, MR. CONNORS.
SCRIBBLE SCRIBBLE
I'LL HAVE TO NOTE THAT YOU TRIED.
BILLY, LOOK AT ME. I WOULD NEVER HURT YOU...
I'VE GOT A GOOD JOB NOW...IN A FEW MONTHS I'LL BE ABLE TO HIRE A LAWYER AND GET YOU BACK, BUT YOU'VE GOT TO TRUST ME.
THE LIZARD IS GONE, BILLY.
ME BEING HERE PROVES THAT--REPTILES DON'T REAR THEIR YOUNG...
WAIT. THAT'S NOT... WHAT I'M TRYING TO SAY IS LOSING YOU WOULD KILL ME, BILLY.
SCRIBBLE SCRIBBLE
YOU'RE USING MANIPULATIVE LANGUAGE. THIS VISIT IS OVER.
I-I'M TELLING MY SON WHAT HE MEANS TO ME!
BILLY, IS HE MAKING YOU UNCOMFORTABLE?
YES.
BILLEEE

SOME GIRL PLAYING WITH YOUR HEART ON THE OTHER LINE?

NO-- I WAS TALKING TO MY *AUNT.*

EH, MY STATEMENT COULD STILL BE ACCURATE.

LISTEN, HARRY, THAT'S A WHOLE OTHER THING--

--WHICH MIGHT INVOLVE HORMONES--

CAN WE CHANGE THE SUBJECT?

SURE THING, BUDDY. *YOU* CALLED ME, WE CAN TALK ABOUT WHATEVER YOU WANT.

UH, I CALLED *MJ* AND *YOU* ANSWERED THE PHONE.

WHICH IS ALWAYS WEIRD.

HEY, ME AND MJ ARE ROOMMATES NOW...WE'RE A TEAM.

TWO PEAS IN A POD.

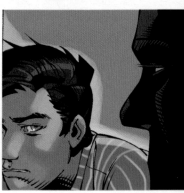

OH--I MEAN... NOT LIKE *THAT* OF COURSE.

...COME ON.

LET'S CHANGE THE SUBJECT. THIS IS *YOUR* DAY, PARKER... WHAT'S UP?

I'VE BEEN, *"HAVING FUN"* WITH THIS GIRL--

--HER WORDS, NOT MINE--

AND SHE'S TOLD ME IN NO UNCERTAIN TERMS THAT IT'S NOT GOING TO GO FARTHER. AND I HONESTLY THINK THE ONLY REASON I HAVEN'T ASKED CARLIE, ON A *"DATE"* DATE IS THIS GIRL, AND--

GO ON...

WAIT, WHAT ARE YOU DOING WITH MY PHONE?

YOU MEAN WHAT ARE *YOU* DOING? ASKING CARLIE ON A *"DATE."*

GIVE ME THAT!

IT'S FOR YOUR OWN GOOD!

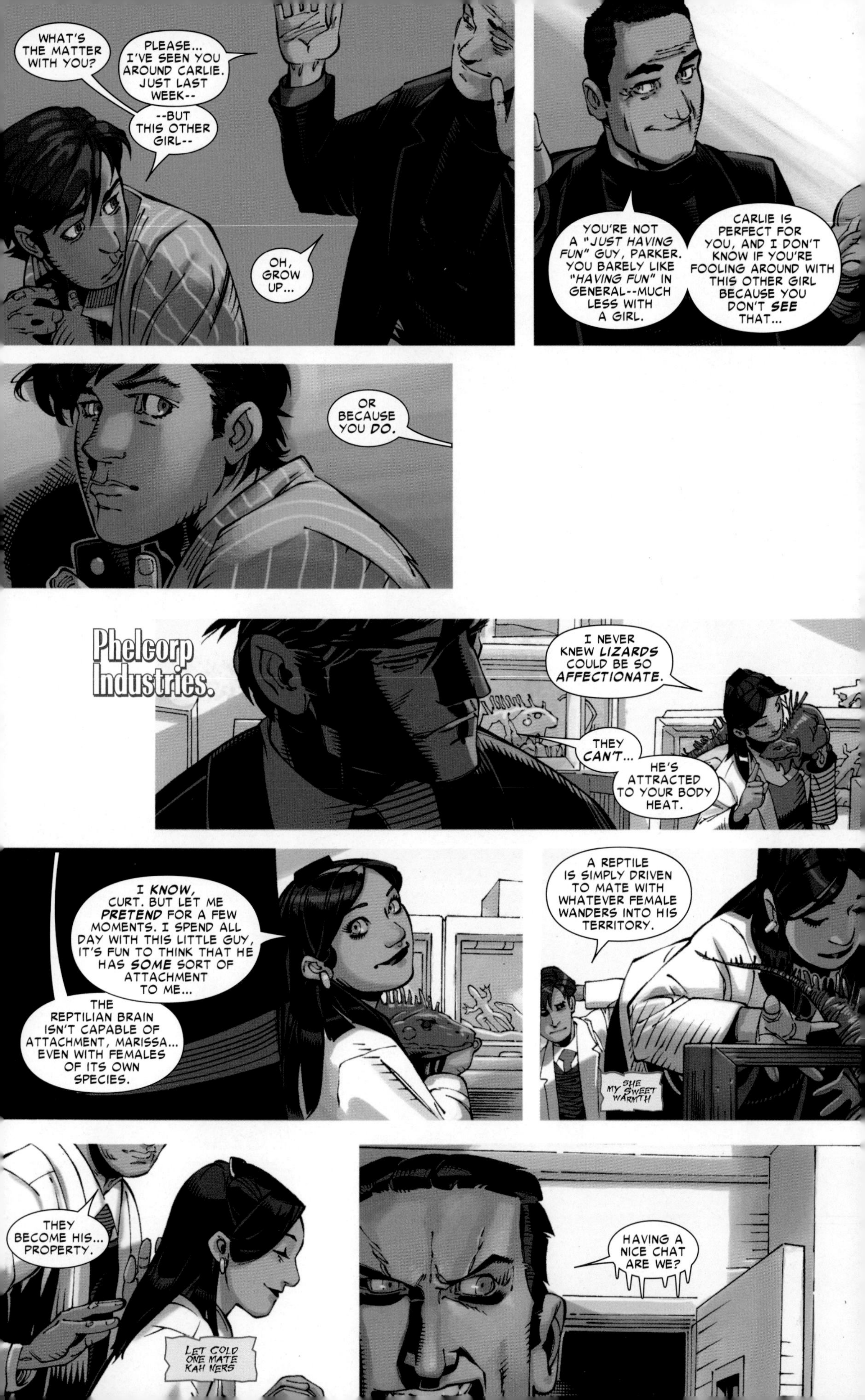
WHAT'S THE MATTER WITH YOU?
PLEASE... I'VE SEEN YOU AROUND CARLIE. JUST LAST WEEK--
--BUT THIS OTHER GIRL--
OH, GROW UP...
YOU'RE NOT A "JUST HAVING FUN" GUY, PARKER. YOU BARELY LIKE "HAVING FUN" IN GENERAL--MUCH LESS WITH A GIRL.
CARLIE IS PERFECT FOR YOU, AND I DON'T KNOW IF YOU'RE FOOLING AROUND WITH THIS OTHER GIRL BECAUSE YOU DON'T SEE THAT...
OR BECAUSE YOU DO.
Phelcorp Industries.
I NEVER KNEW LIZARDS COULD BE SO AFFECTIONATE.
THEY CAN'T...
HE'S ATTRACTED TO YOUR BODY HEAT.
I KNOW, CURT. BUT LET ME PRETEND FOR A FEW MOMENTS. I SPEND ALL DAY WITH THIS LITTLE GUY, IT'S FUN TO THINK THAT HE HAS SOME SORT OF ATTACHMENT TO ME...
THE REPTILIAN BRAIN ISN'T CAPABLE OF ATTACHMENT, MARISSA... EVEN WITH FEMALES OF ITS OWN SPECIES.
A REPTILE IS SIMPLY DRIVEN TO MATE WITH WHATEVER FEMALE WANDERS INTO HIS TERRITORY.
SHE MY SWEET WARMTH
THEY BECOME HIS... PROPERTY.
LET COLD ONE MATE KAH NERS
HAVING A NICE CHAT ARE WE?

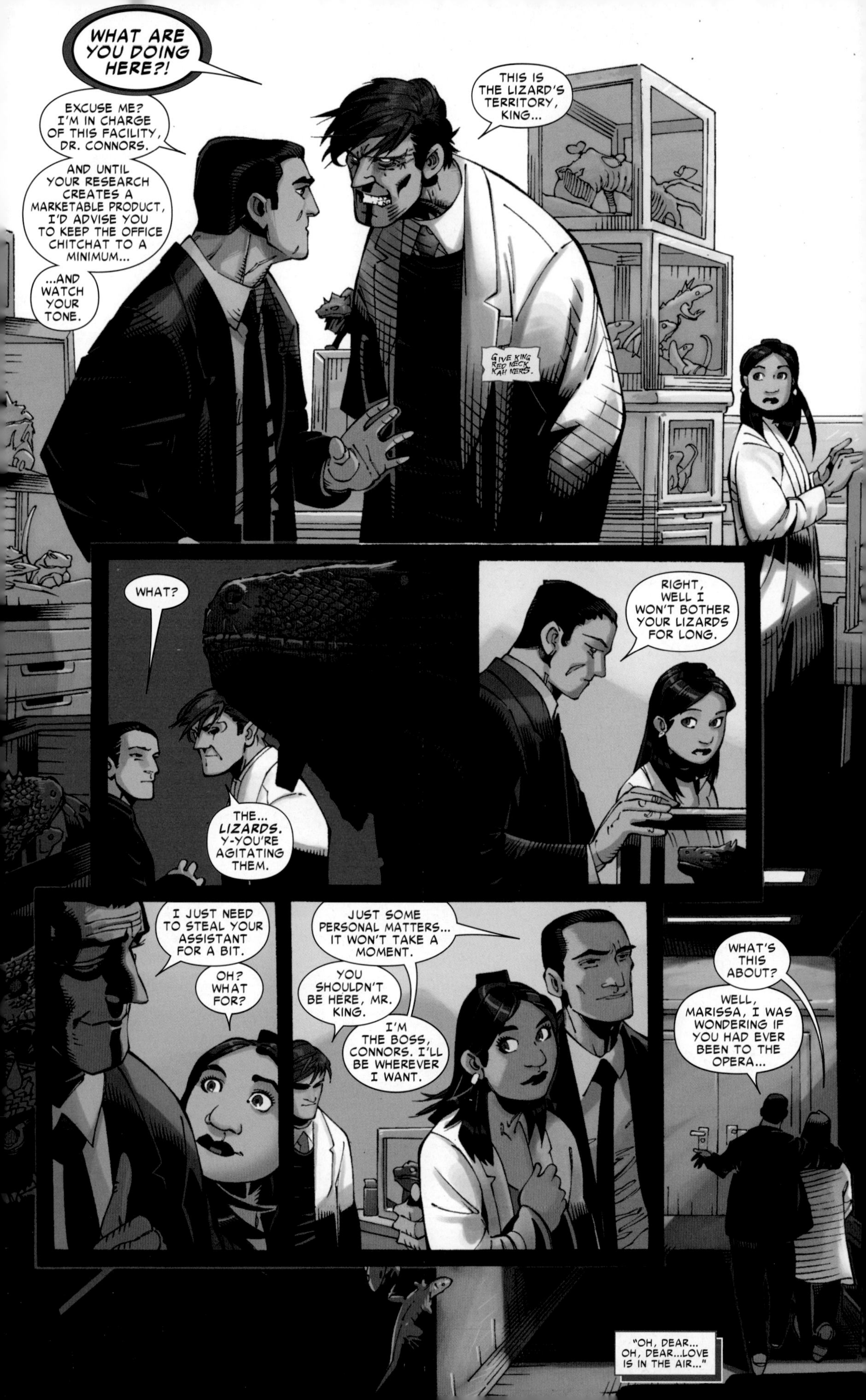
WHAT ARE YOU DOING HERE?!
EXCUSE ME? I'M IN CHARGE OF THIS FACILITY, DR. CONNORS.
AND UNTIL YOUR RESEARCH CREATES A MARKETABLE PRODUCT, I'D ADVISE YOU TO KEEP THE OFFICE CHITCHAT TO A MINIMUM...
...AND WATCH YOUR TONE.
THIS IS THE LIZARD'S TERRITORY, KING...
GIVE KING RED NECK KAHNERS
WHAT?
THE... LIZARDS. Y-YOU'RE AGITATING THEM.
RIGHT, WELL I WON'T BOTHER YOUR LIZARDS FOR LONG.
I JUST NEED TO STEAL YOUR ASSISTANT FOR A BIT.
OH? WHAT FOR?
JUST SOME PERSONAL MATTERS... IT WON'T TAKE A MOMENT.
YOU SHOULDN'T BE HERE, MR. KING.
I'M THE BOSS, CONNORS. I'LL BE WHEREVER I WANT.
WHAT'S THIS ABOUT?
WELL, MARISSA, I WAS WONDERING IF YOU HAD EVER BEEN TO THE OPERA...
"OH, DEAR... OH, DEAR...LOVE IS IN THE AIR..."

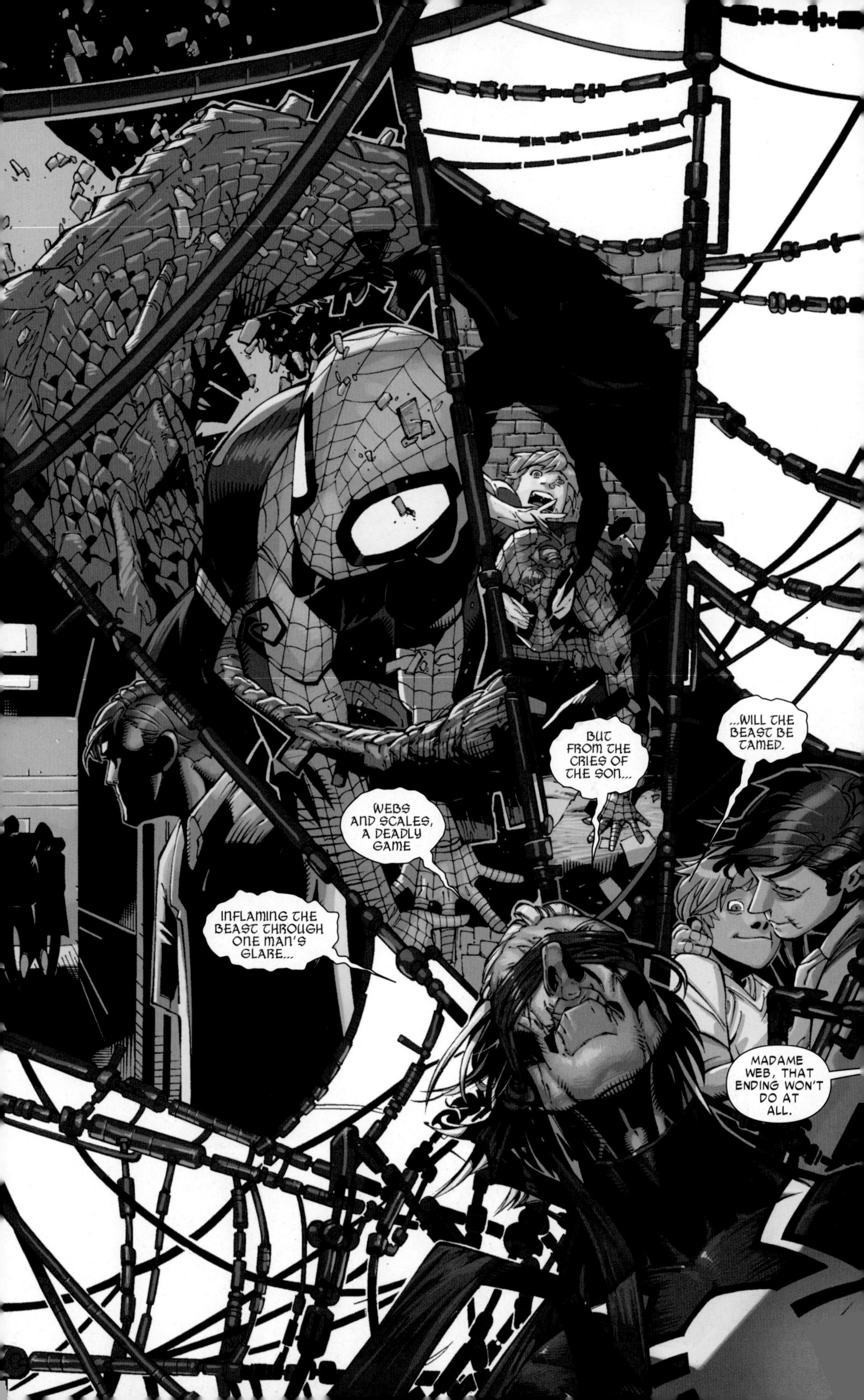

INFLAMING THE BEAST THROUGH ONE MAN'S GLARE...
WEBS AND SCALES, A DEADLY GAME
BUT FROM THE CRIES OF THE SON...
...WILL THE BEAST BE TAMED.
MADAME WEB, THAT ENDING WON'T DO AT ALL.

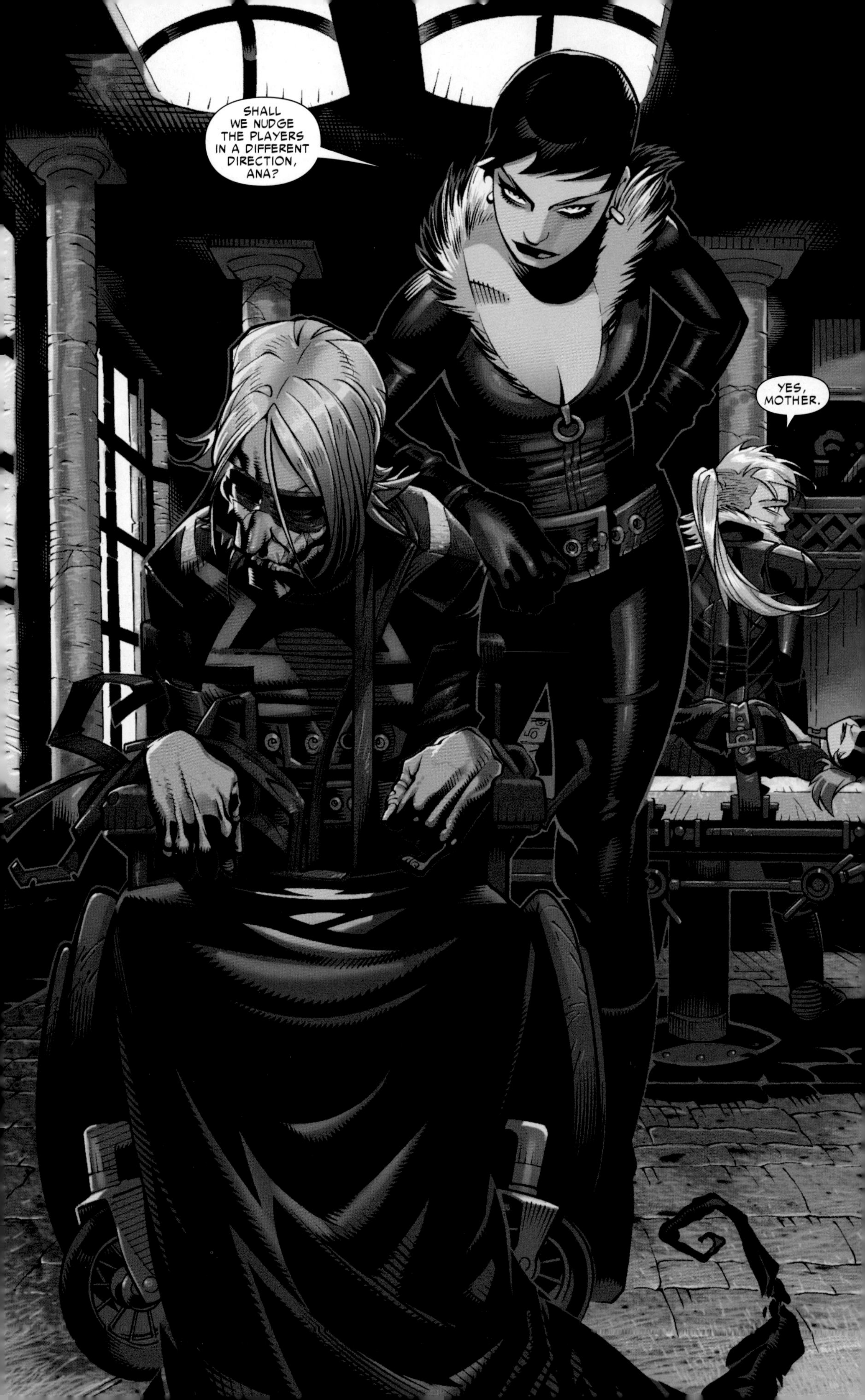
SHALL WE NUDGE THE PLAYERS IN A DIFFERENT DIRECTION, ANA?
YES, MOTHER.

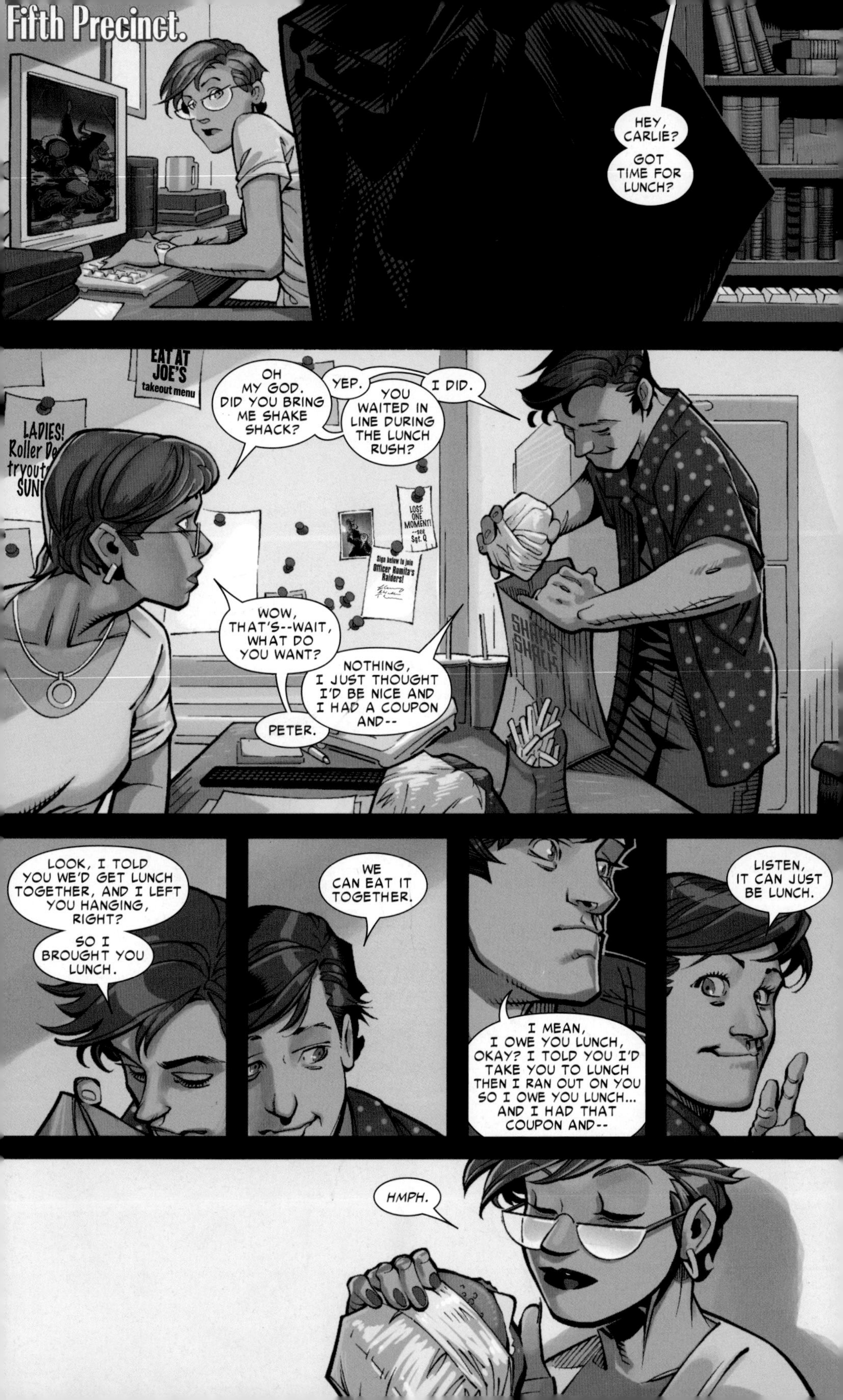

Fifth Precinct.
HEY, CARLIE? GOT TIME FOR LUNCH?
EAT AT JOE'S takeout menu
LADIES!
OH MY GOD. DID YOU BRING ME SHAKE SHACK?
YEP.
I DID.
YOU WAITED IN LINE DURING THE LUNCH RUSH?
LOST: ONE MOMENT! --see Sgt. Q.
Sign below to join Officer Romita's Raiders!
SHAKE SHACK
WOW, THAT'S--WAIT, WHAT DO YOU WANT?
NOTHING, I JUST THOUGHT I'D BE NICE AND I HAD A COUPON AND--
PETER.
LOOK, I TOLD YOU WE'D GET LUNCH TOGETHER, AND I LEFT YOU HANGING, RIGHT?
SO I BROUGHT YOU LUNCH.
WE CAN EAT IT TOGETHER.
I MEAN, I OWE YOU LUNCH, OKAY? I TOLD YOU I'D TAKE YOU TO LUNCH THEN I RAN OUT ON YOU SO I OWE YOU LUNCH... AND I HAD THAT COUPON AND--
LISTEN, IT CAN JUST BE LUNCH.
HMPH.

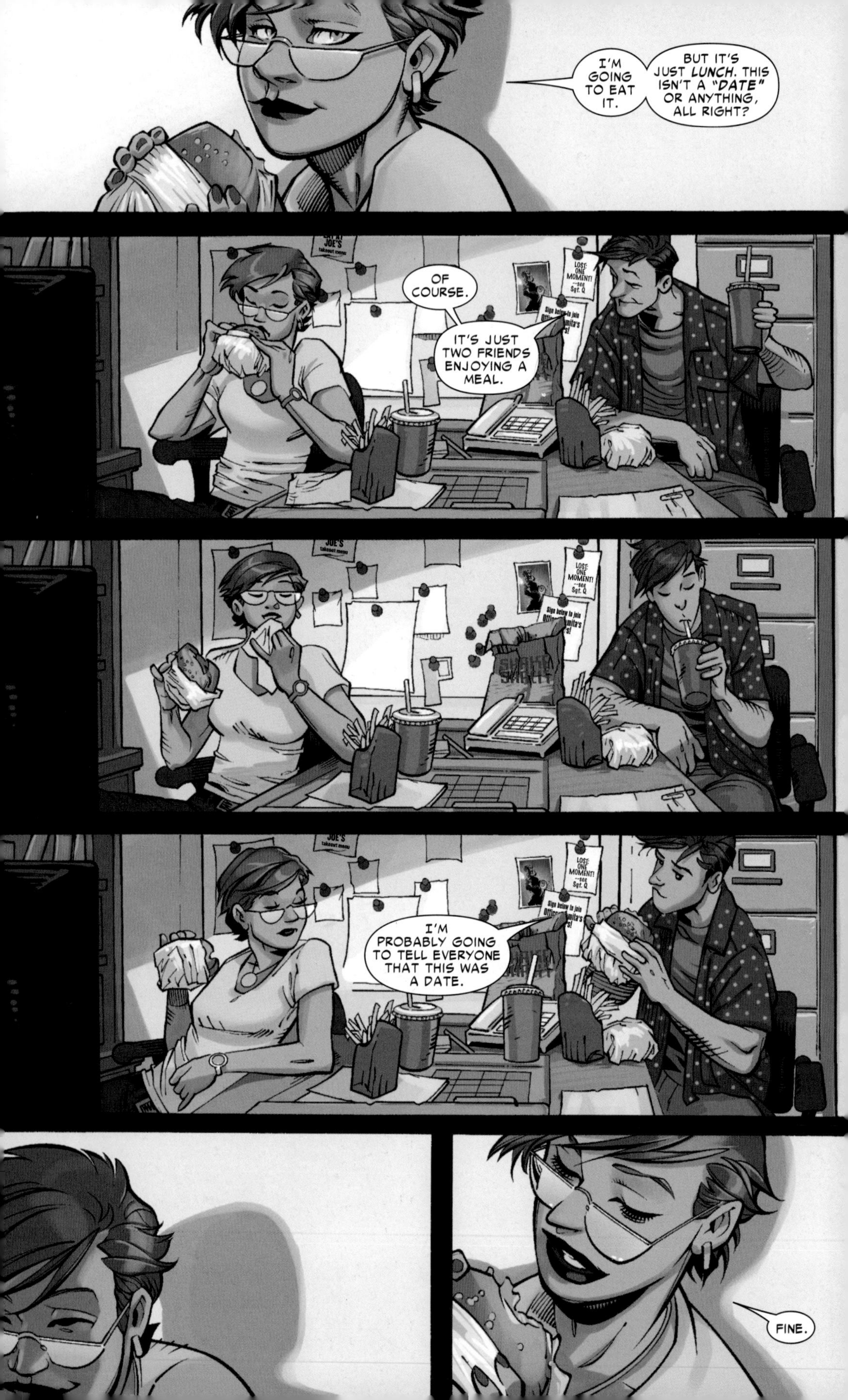
I'M GOING TO EAT IT.
BUT IT'S JUST LUNCH. THIS ISN'T A "DATE" OR ANYTHING, ALL RIGHT?
JOE'S takeout menu
LOST: ONE MOMENT! --see Sgt. Q
OF COURSE.
IT'S JUST TWO FRIENDS ENJOYING A MEAL.
I'M PROBABLY GOING TO TELL EVERYONE THAT THIS WAS A DATE.
FINE.

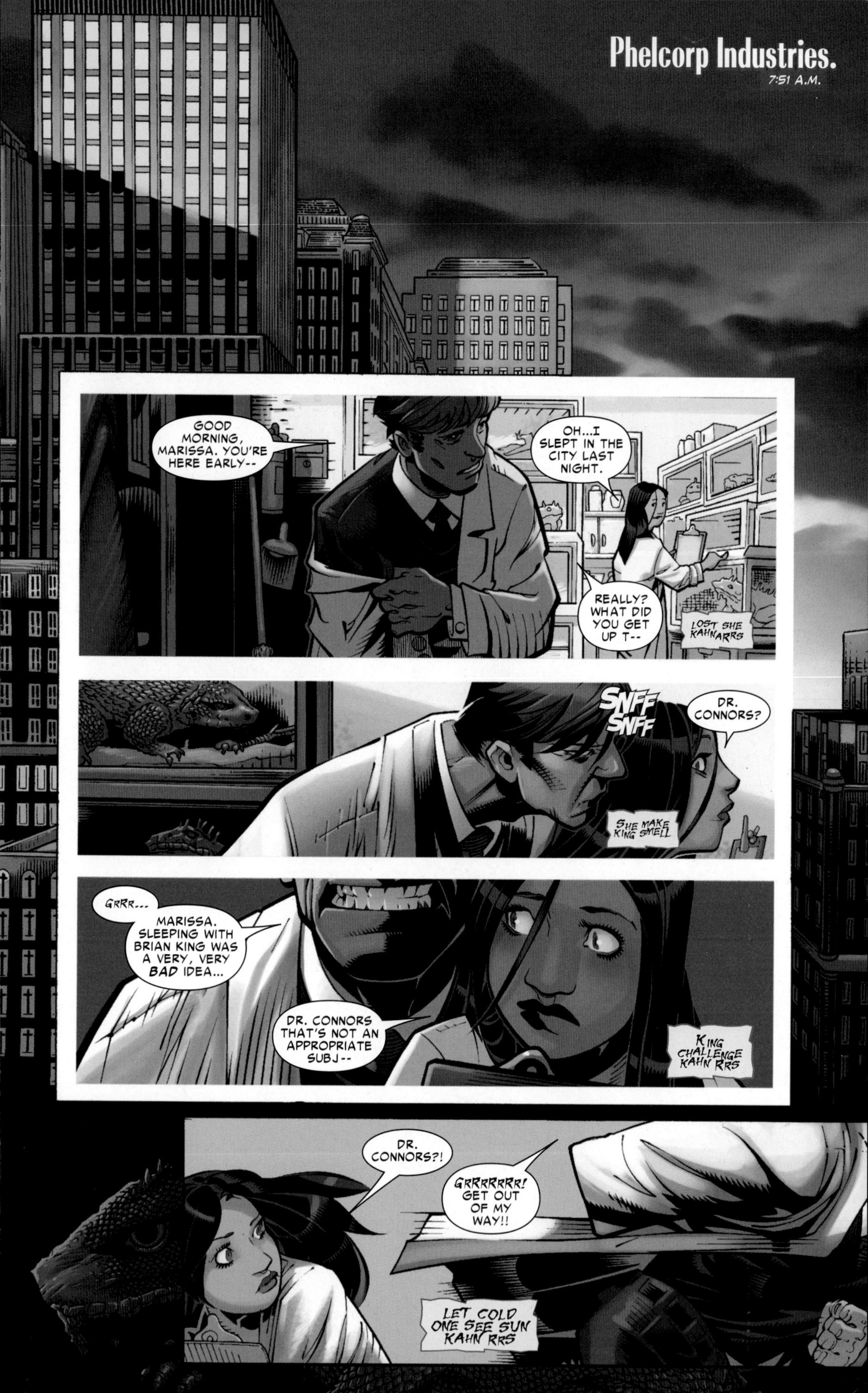
Phelcorp Industries.
7:51 A.M.
GOOD MORNING, MARISSA. YOU'RE HERE EARLY--
OH...I SLEPT IN THE CITY LAST NIGHT.
REALLY? WHAT DID YOU GET UP T--
LOST SHE KAHNARRS
SNFF SNFF
DR. CONNORS?
SHE MAKE KING SMELL
GRRR...
MARISSA. SLEEPING WITH BRIAN KING WAS A VERY, VERY BAD IDEA...
DR. CONNORS THAT'S NOT AN APPROPRIATE SUBJ--
KING CHALLENGE KAHN RRS
DR. CONNORS?!
GRRRRRRR! GET OUT OF MY WAY!!
LET COLD ONE SEE SUN KAHN RRS

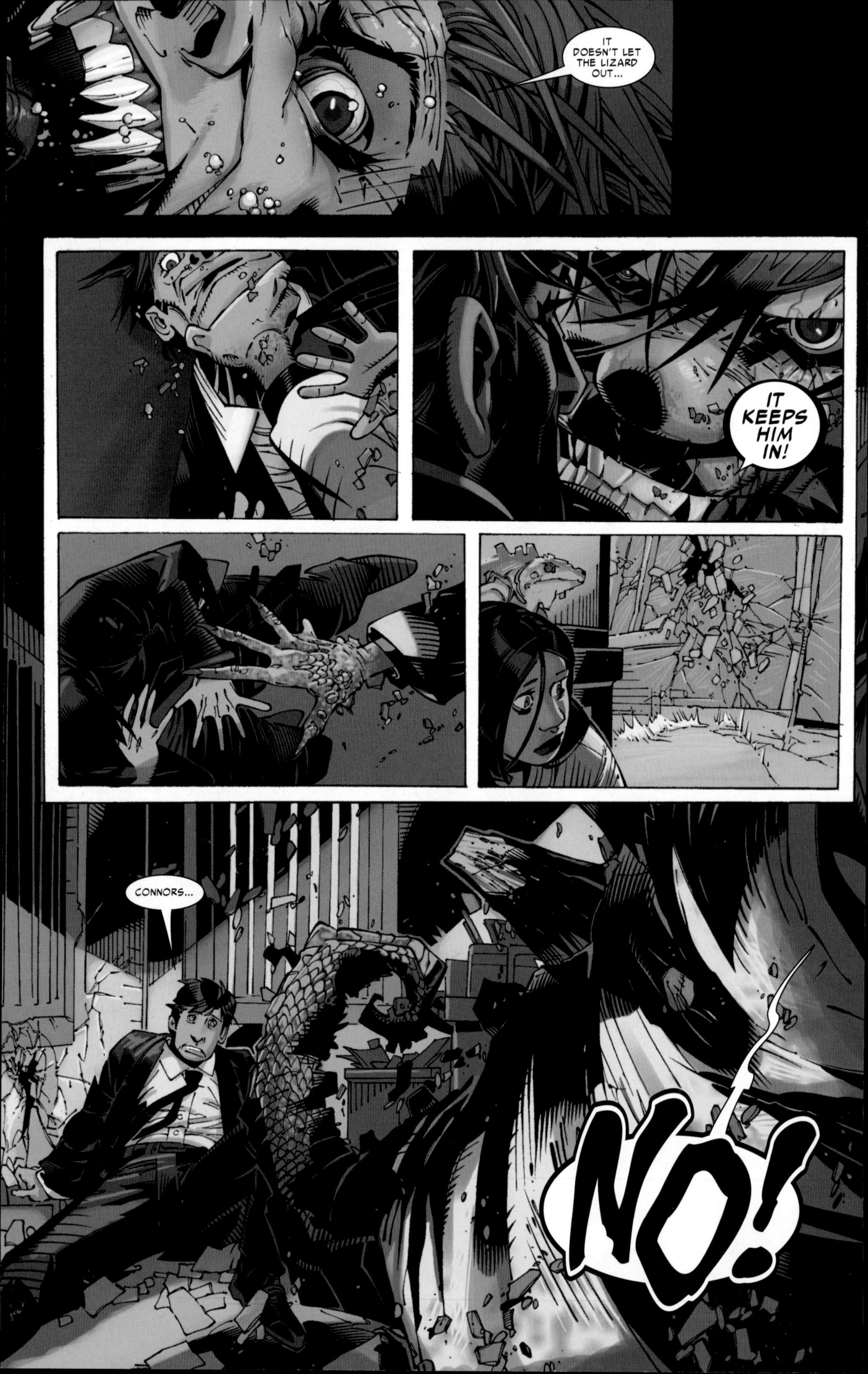
IT DOESN'T LET THE LIZARD OUT...
IT KEEPS HIM IN!
CONNORS...
NO!

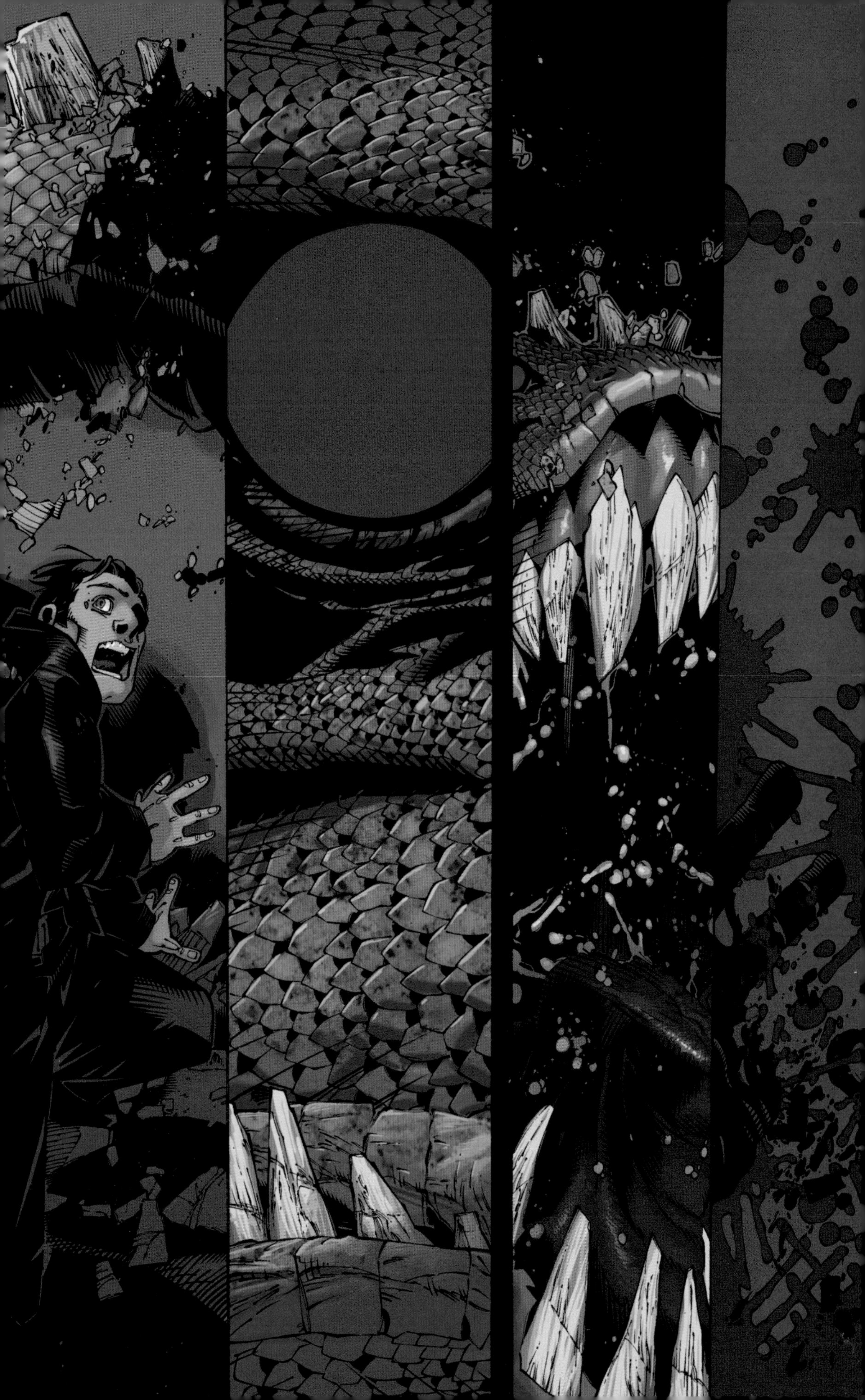

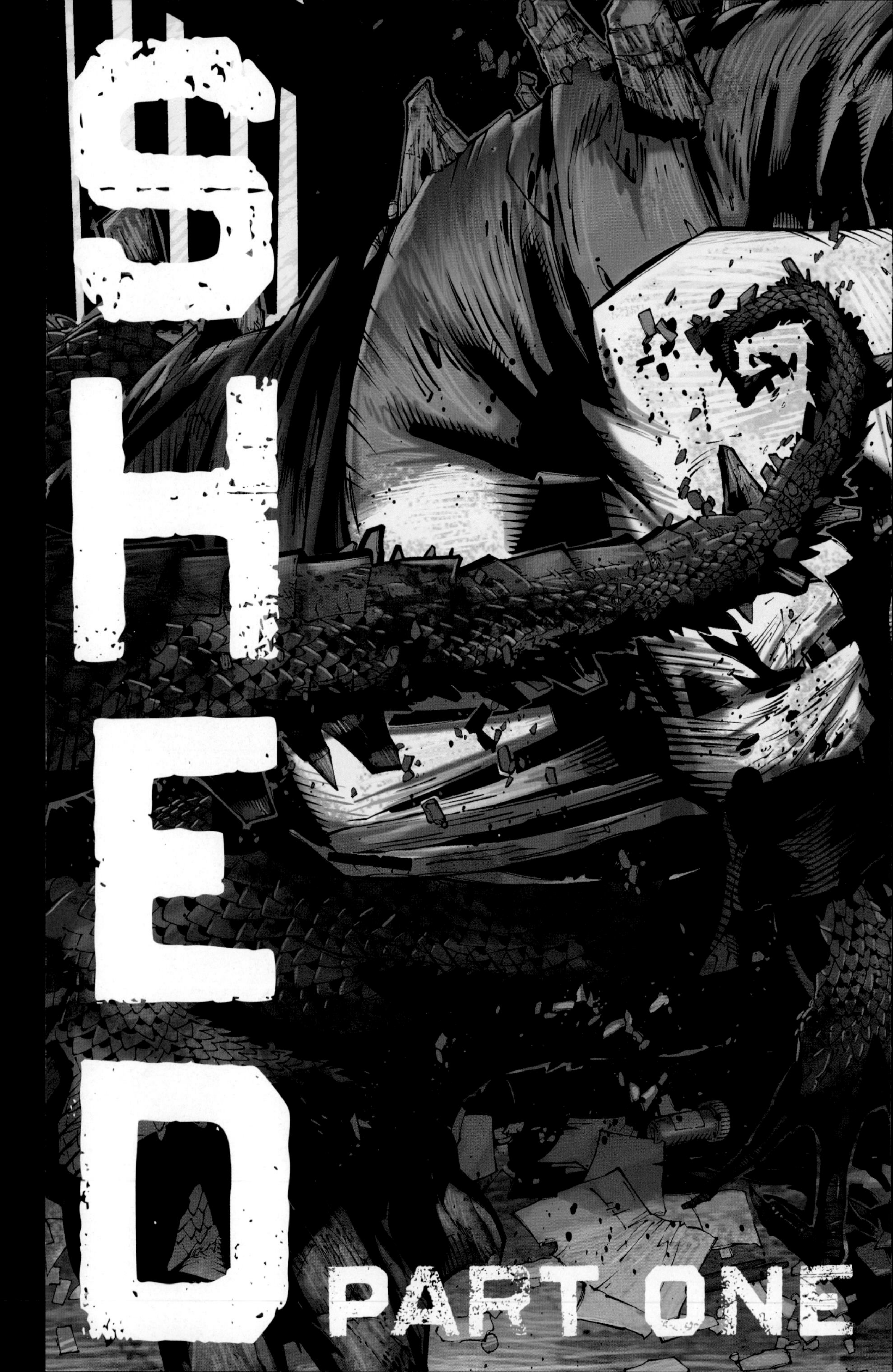
SHED
PART ONE

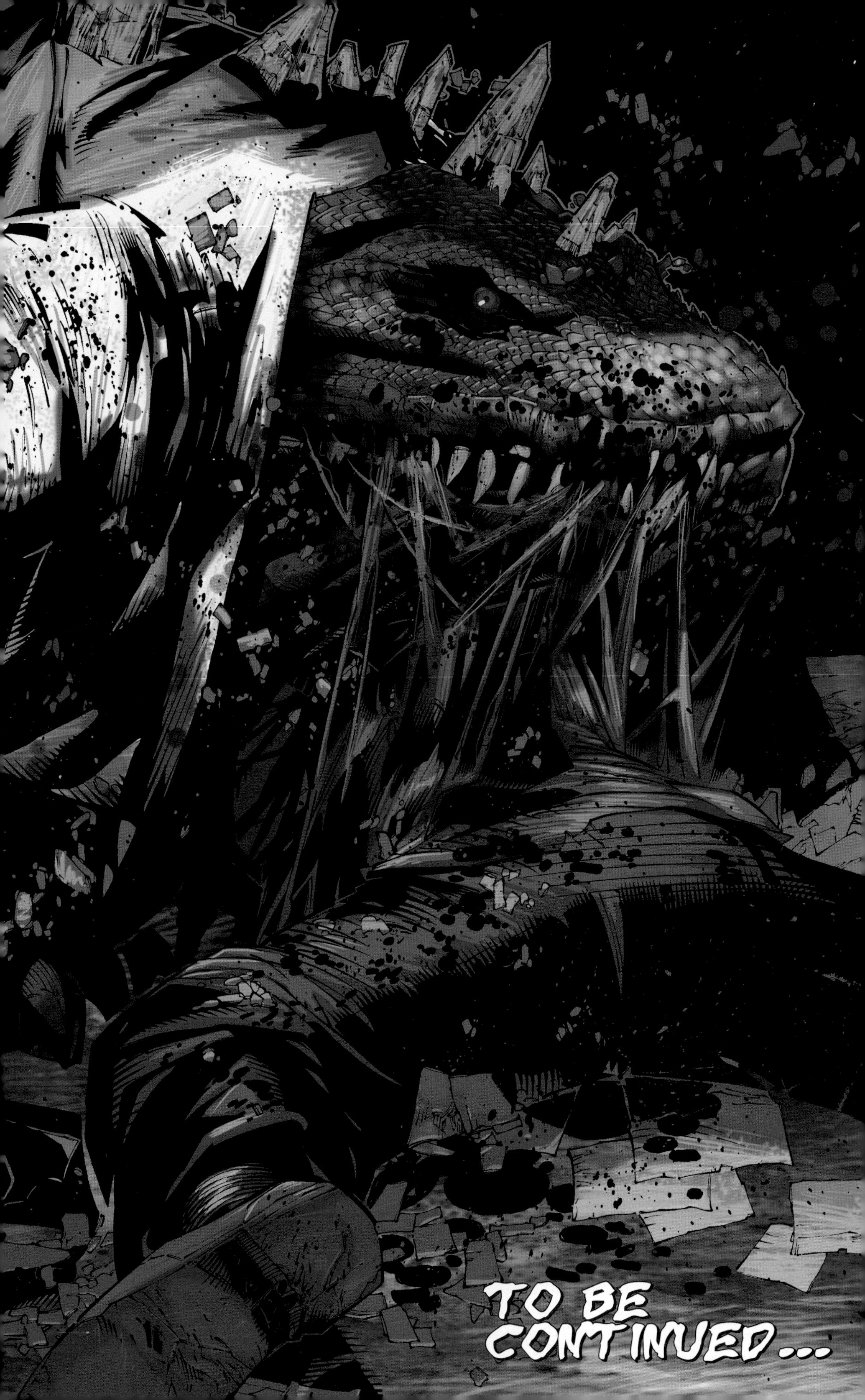
TO BE CONTINUED...

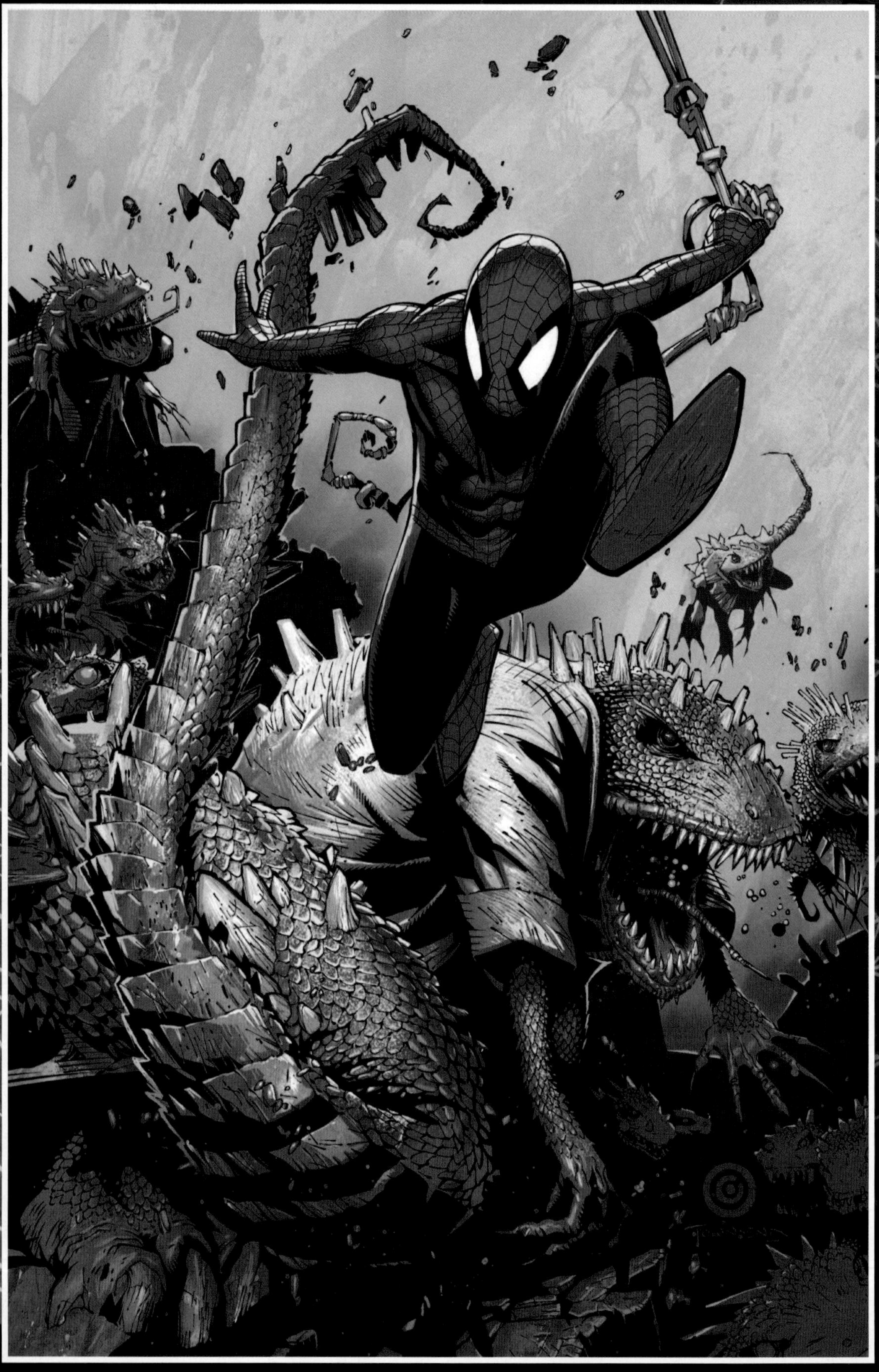

AMAZING SPIDER-MAN #631
COVER BY CHRIS BACHALO & TIM TOWNSEND

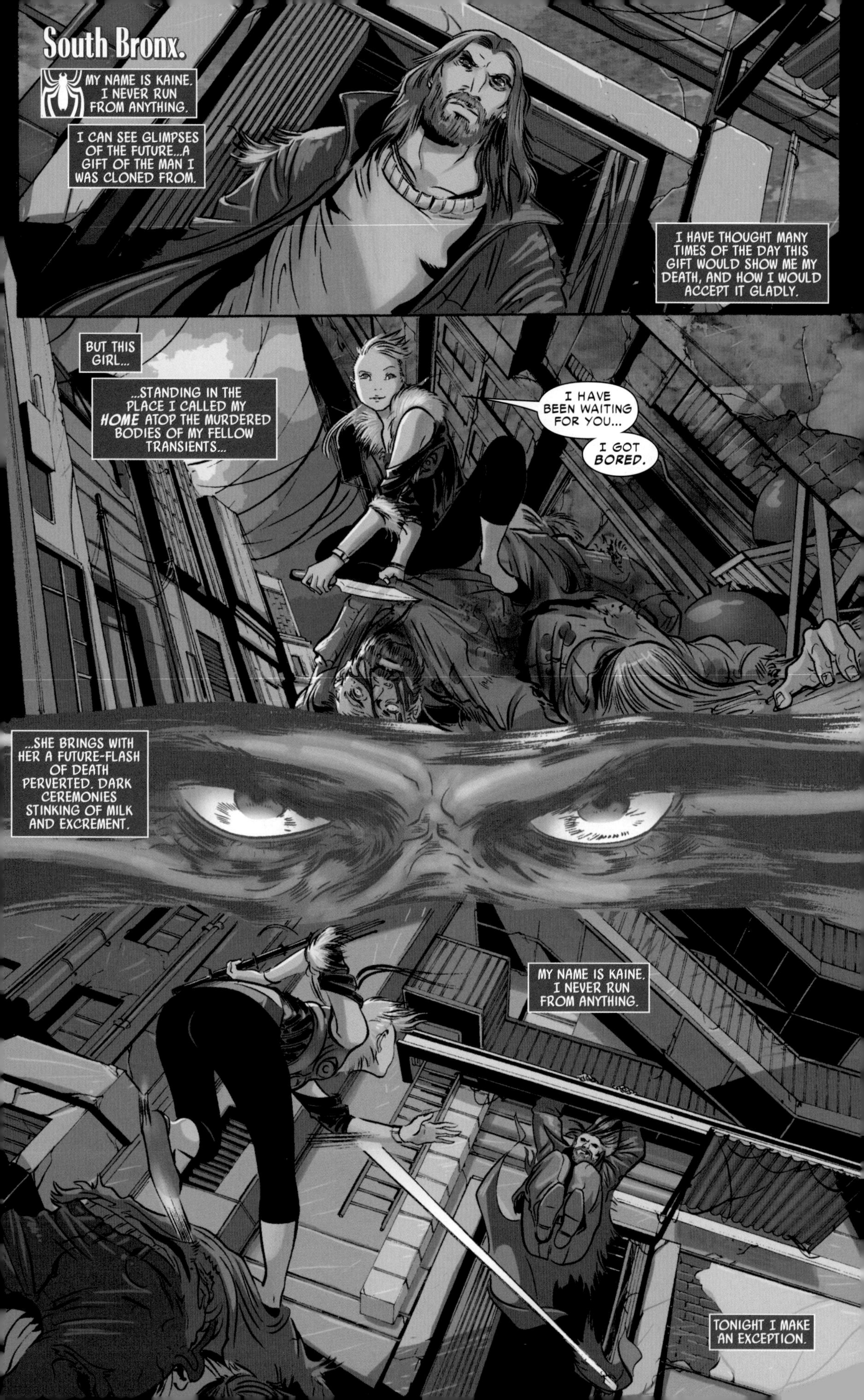
South Bronx.
MY NAME IS KAINE. I NEVER RUN FROM ANYTHING.
I CAN SEE GLIMPSES OF THE FUTURE...A GIFT OF THE MAN I WAS CLONED FROM.
I HAVE THOUGHT MANY TIMES OF THE DAY THIS GIFT WOULD SHOW ME MY DEATH, AND HOW I WOULD ACCEPT IT GLADLY.
BUT THIS GIRL...
...STANDING IN THE PLACE I CALLED MY HOME ATOP THE MURDERED BODIES OF MY FELLOW TRANSIENTS...
I HAVE BEEN WAITING FOR YOU...
I GOT BORED.
...SHE BRINGS WITH HER A FUTURE-FLASH OF DEATH PERVERTED. DARK CEREMONIES STINKING OF MILK AND EXCREMENT.
MY NAME IS KAINE. I NEVER RUN FROM ANYTHING.
TONIGHT I MAKE AN EXCEPTION.

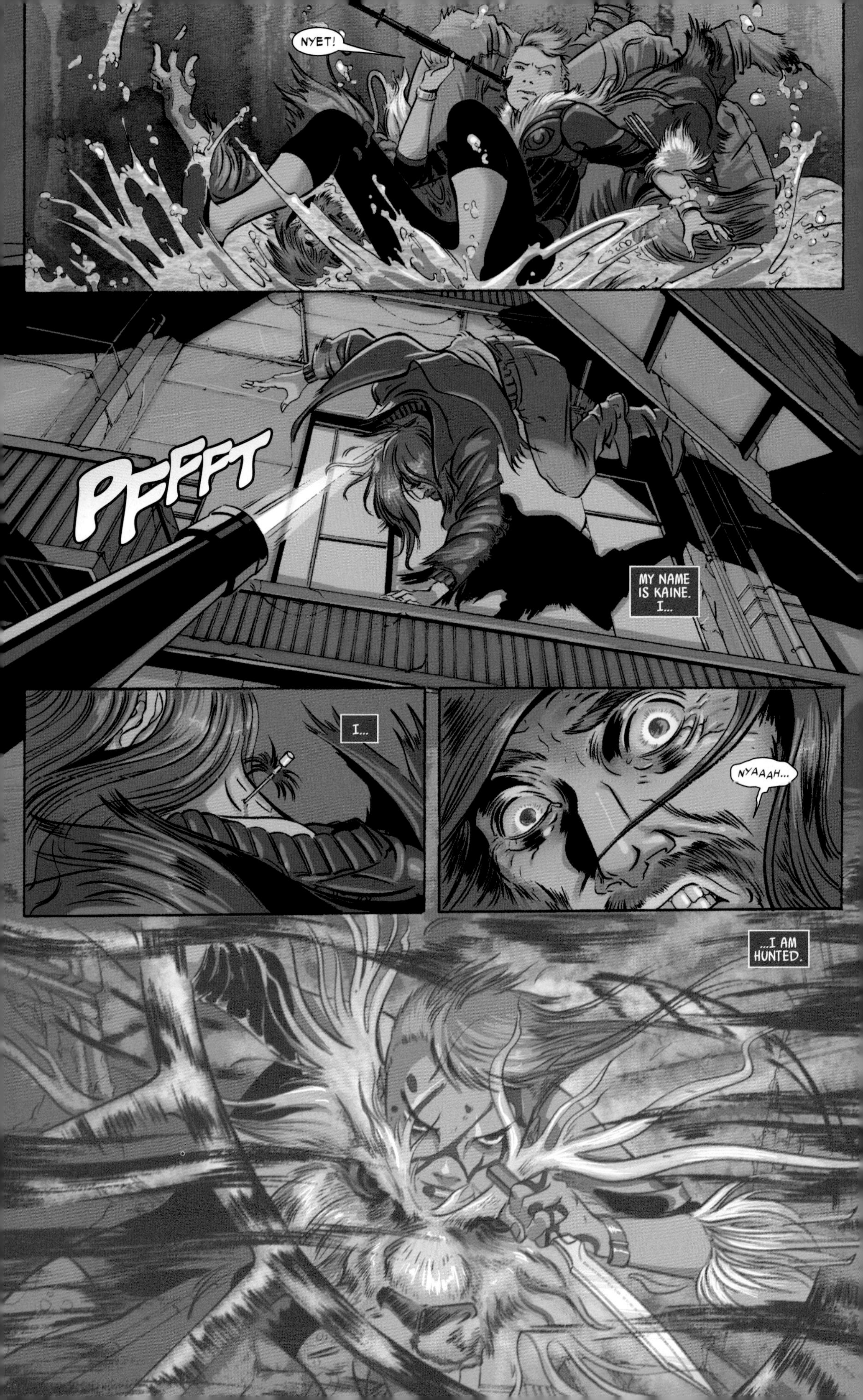
NYET!
PFFFT
MY NAME IS KAINE. I...
I...
NYAAAH...
...I AM HUNTED.

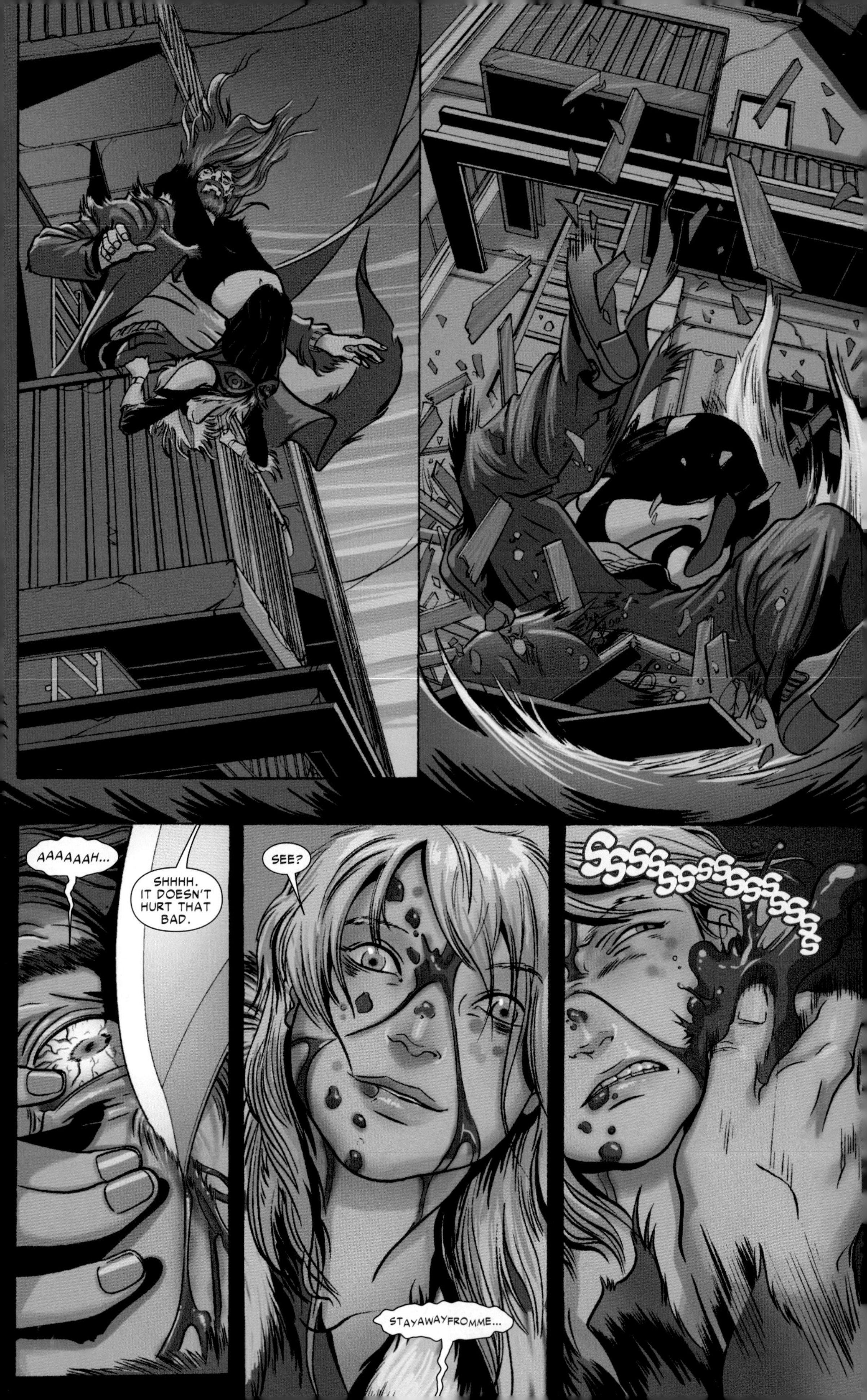
AAAAAAH...
SHHHH. IT DOESN'T HURT THAT BAD.
SEE?
STAYAWAYFROMME...
SSSSSSSSSSSSSSSSS

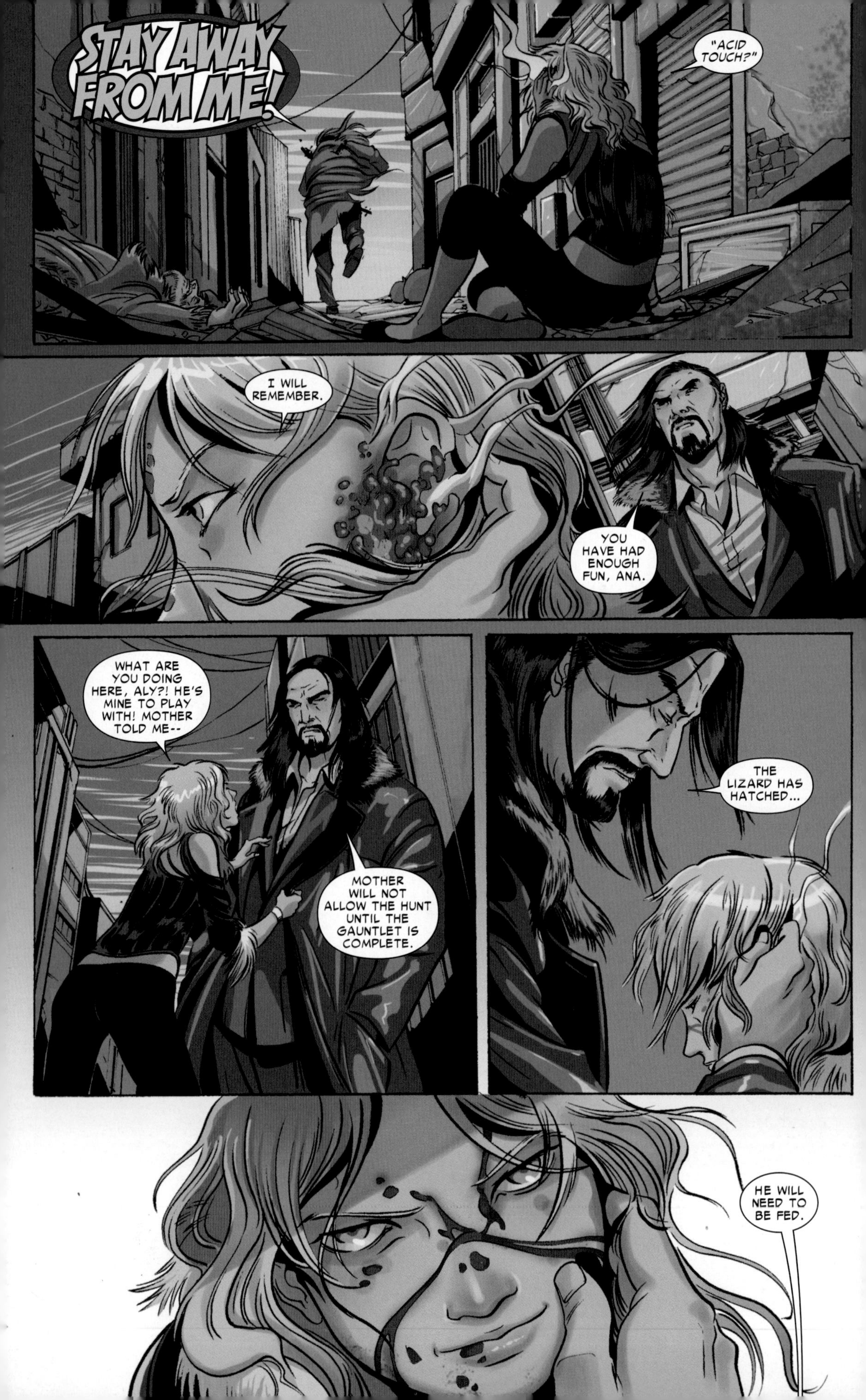
STAY AWAY FROM ME!
"ACID TOUCH?"
I WILL REMEMBER.
YOU HAVE HAD ENOUGH FUN, ANA.
WHAT ARE YOU DOING HERE, ALY?! HE'S MINE TO PLAY WITH! MOTHER TOLD ME--
MOTHER WILL NOT ALLOW THE HUNT UNTIL THE GAUNTLET IS COMPLETE.
THE LIZARD HAS HATCHED...
HE WILL NEED TO BE FED.

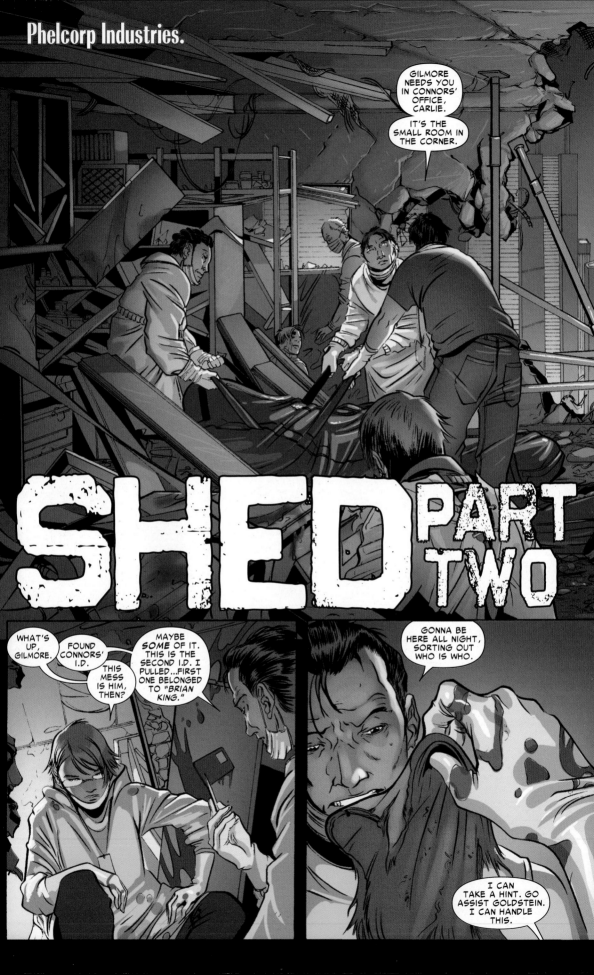

THE DEATH OF CURT CONNORS

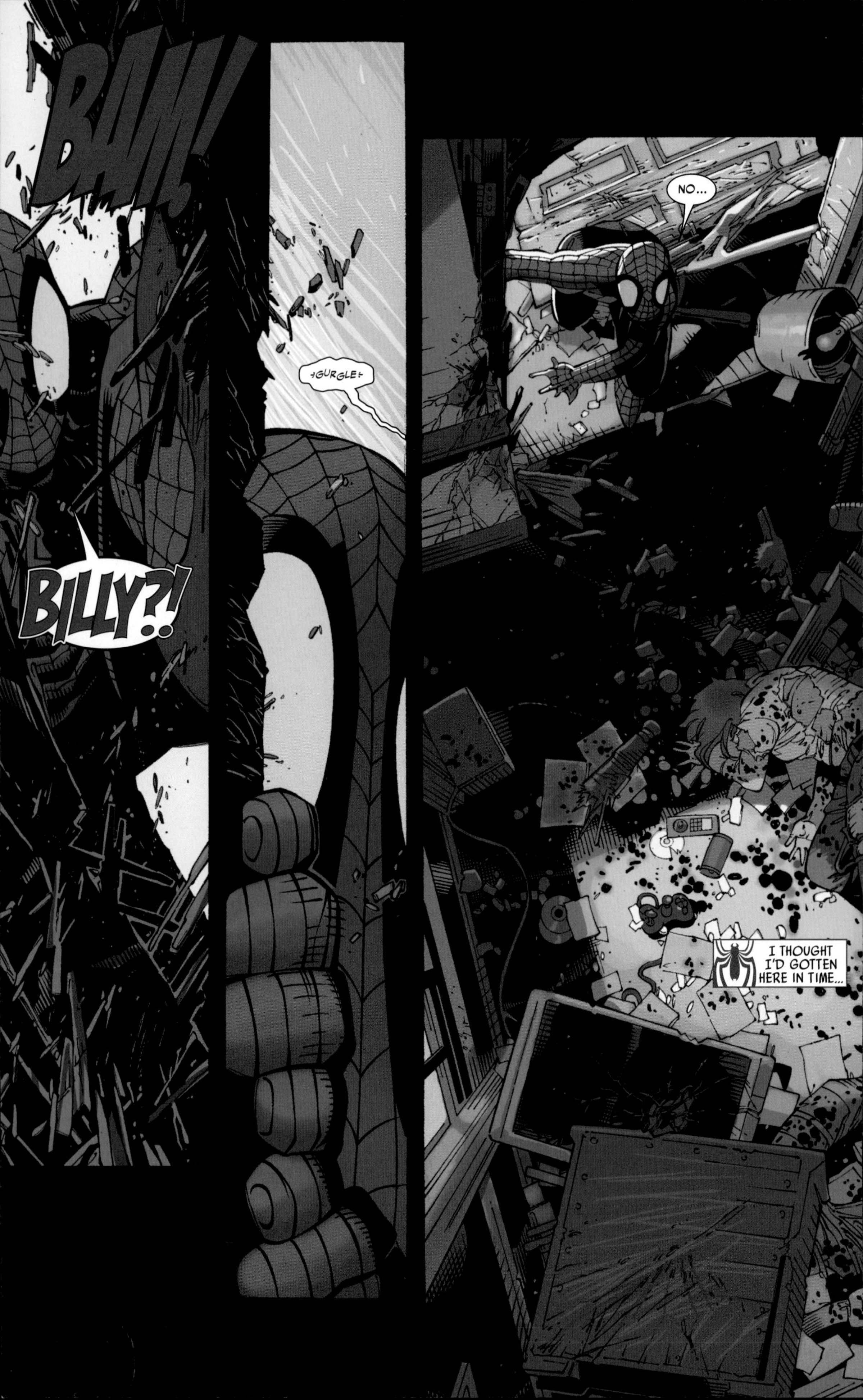
BAM!
BILLY?!
GURGLE
NO...
I THOUGHT I'D GOTTEN HERE IN TIME...

IT'S BETTER THIS WAY. YOU SHOULD BE WITH YOUR FATHER.

FAMILY IS YOUR LEGACY.

DAD?

SSSSSSSSSSSSSSSSSSSS

OH, GOD...

DON'T DO THIS.

NO NO NO.

PUH-PLEASE DON'T, DADDY...

KAH NRRS WANT KILL COLD ONE

KAH NRRS BE RIVAL MALE

NO...

HURF!

NO!

COLD ONE RAID KAH NRRS NEST!

AAGH!!

I'LL DIE BEFORE I LET YOU DO IT!

HNNN... HNNN... HNNN...

COLD ONE EAT KAH NRRS YOUNG!

YA... YOU'RE GOING TO KILL ME, AREN'T YOU?

GUH... GUH...

I KNEW IT...

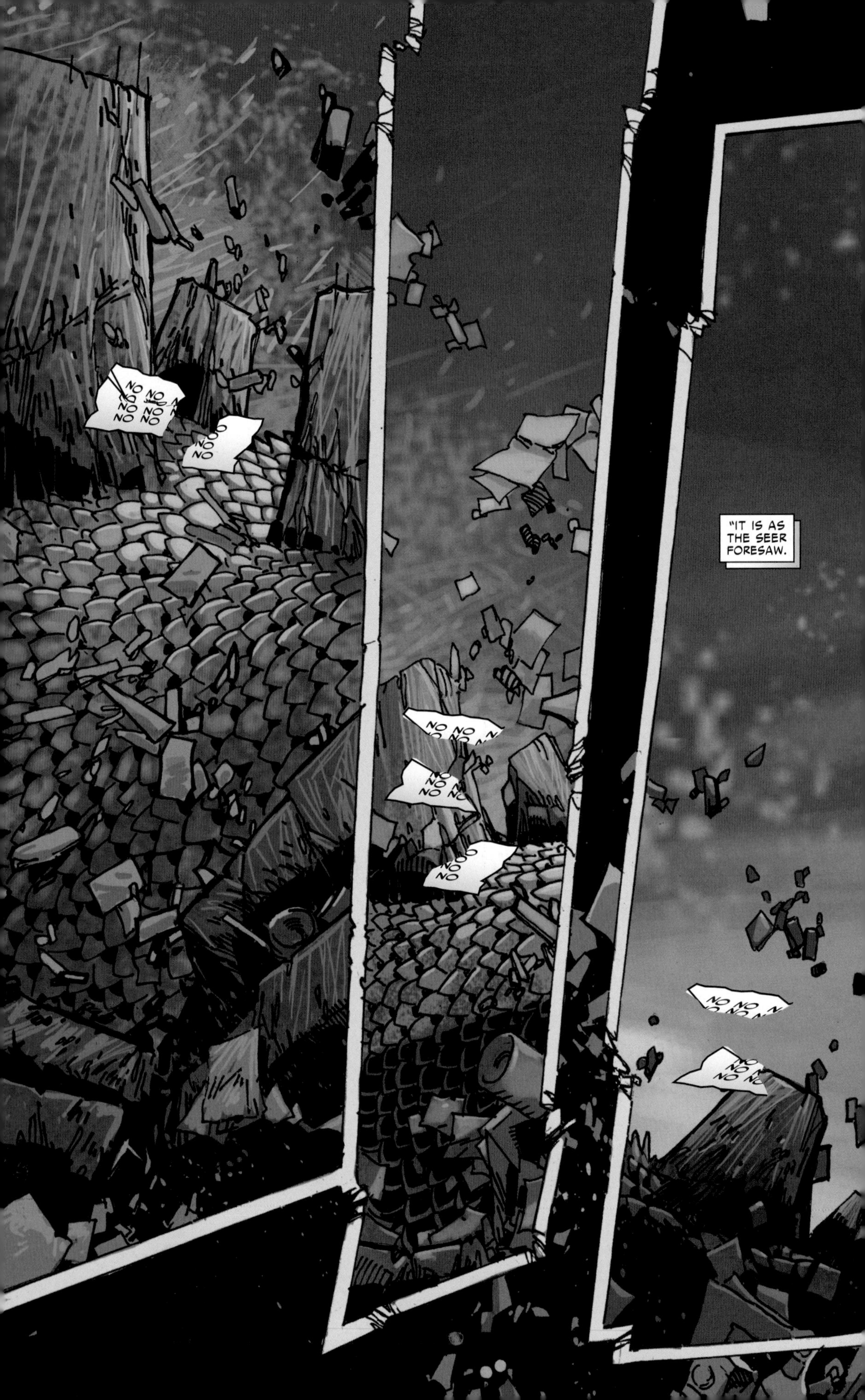
NO NO
NO NO
NO NO
NO
NO
NO NO
NO NO
NO
NO
"IT IS AS THE SEER FORESAW.
NO NO
NO NO

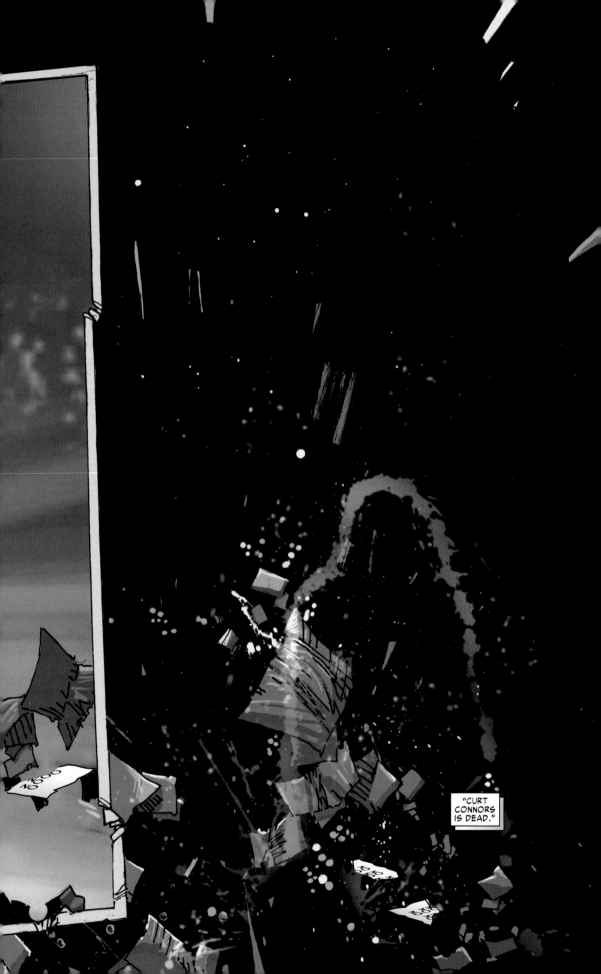

"CURT CONNORS IS DEAD."

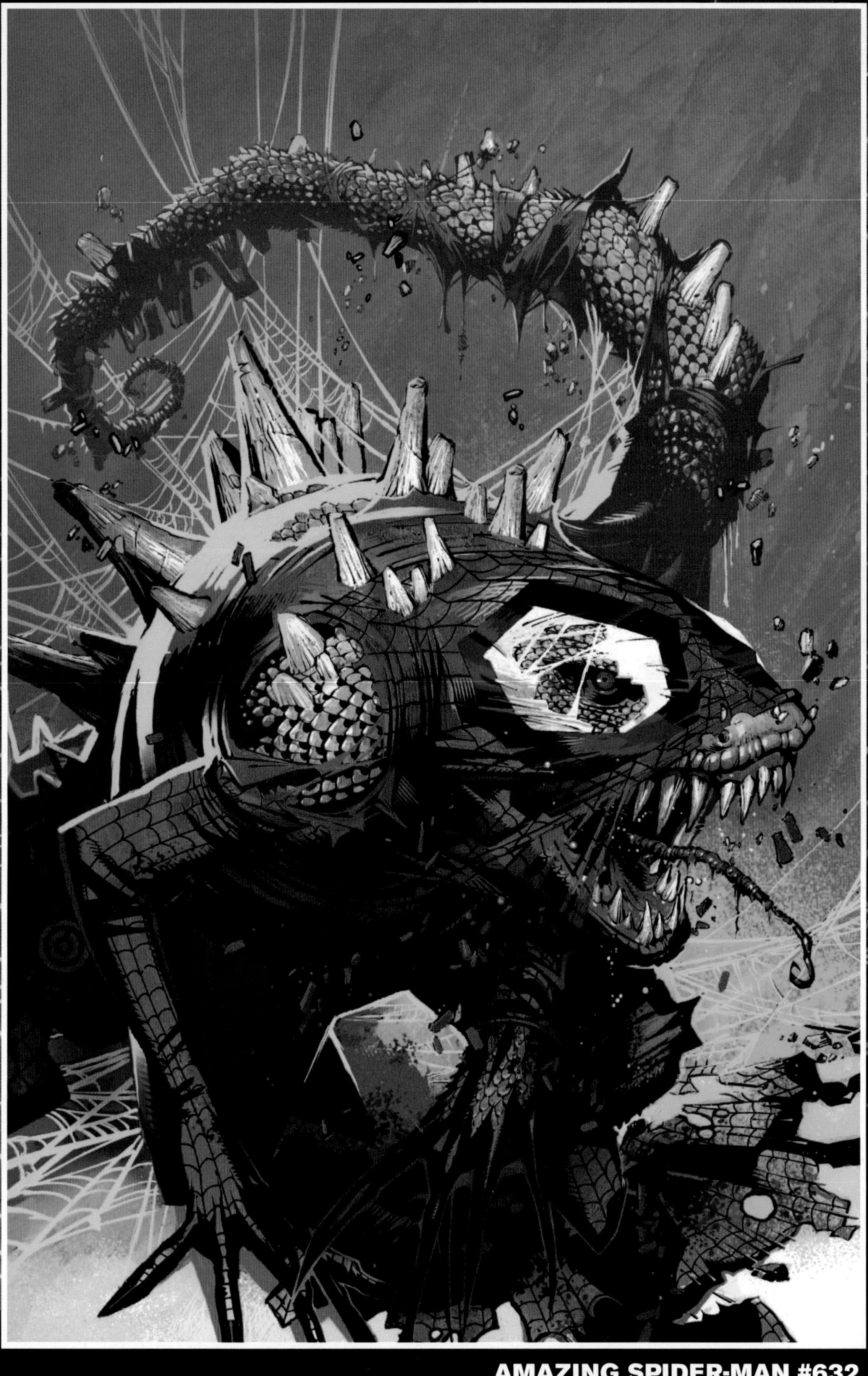

AMAZING SPIDER-MAN #632
COVER BY CHRIS BACHALO & TIM TOWNSEND

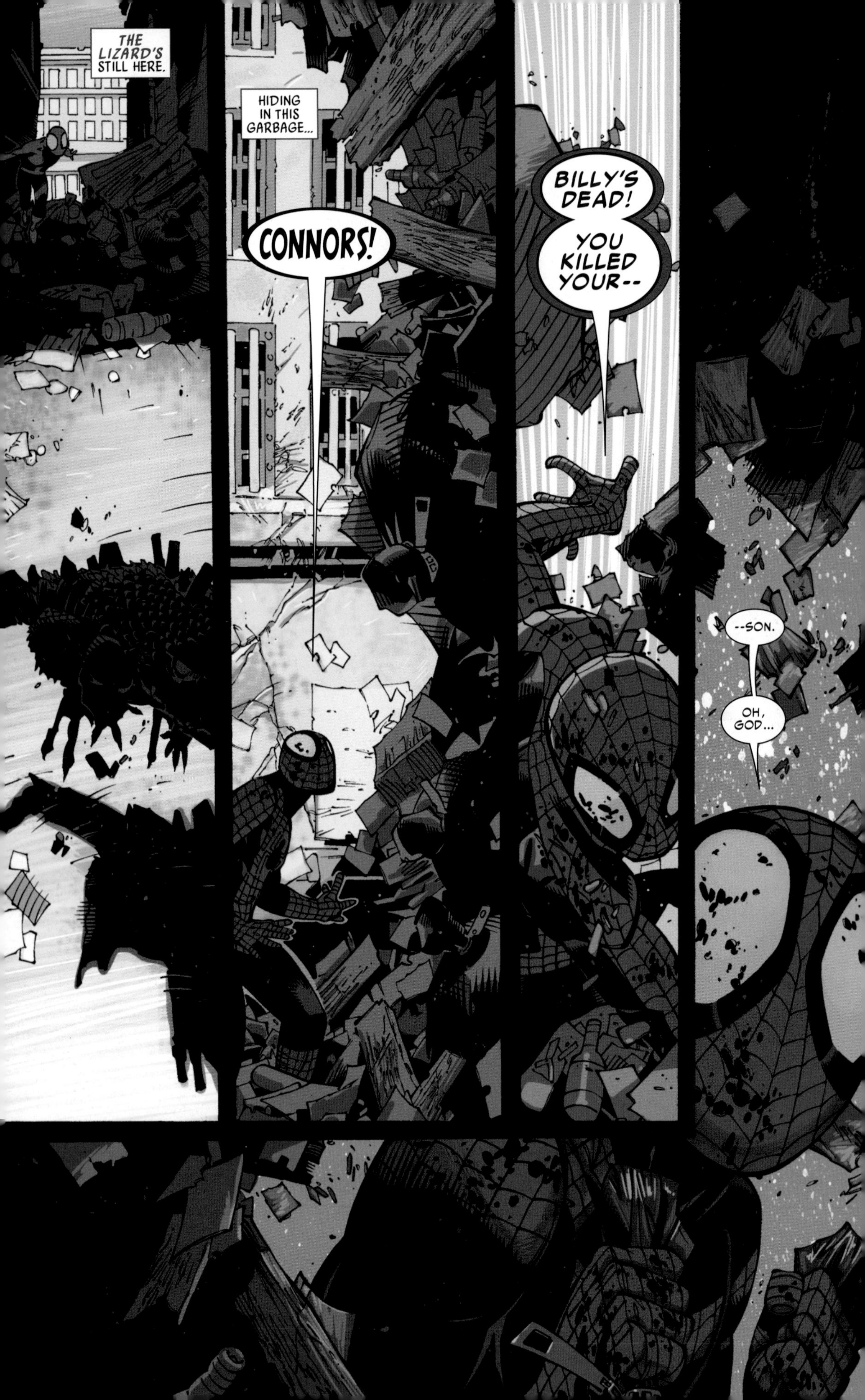
THE LIZARD'S STILL HERE.
HIDING IN THIS GARBAGE...
CONNORS!
BILLY'S DEAD!
YOU KILLED YOUR--
--SON.
OH, GOD...

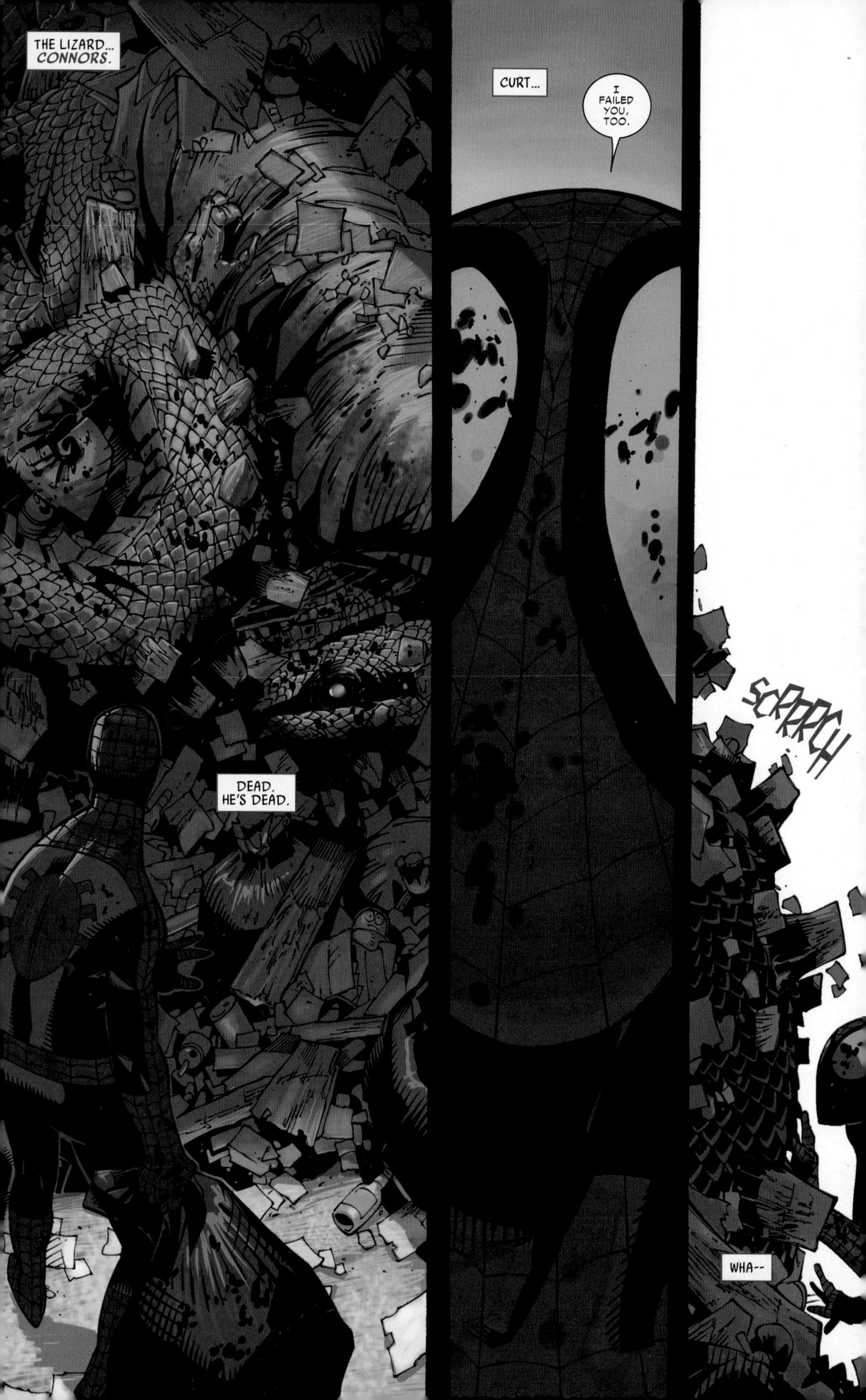
THE LIZARD... CONNORS.
DEAD. HE'S DEAD.
CURT...
I FAILED YOU, TOO.
SCRRRCH
WHA--

KAHN RRS...
IS SHED.

IT...IT'S THE LIZARD BUT...

CURT, LISTEN TO ME...

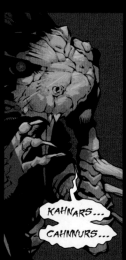

MONKEY BRAIN IS LIZARD HOME NOW. NO MORE KAH NRRS...

KAHNARS...

CAHMNURS...

CONNORS.

YOU...YOU'RE TALKING...

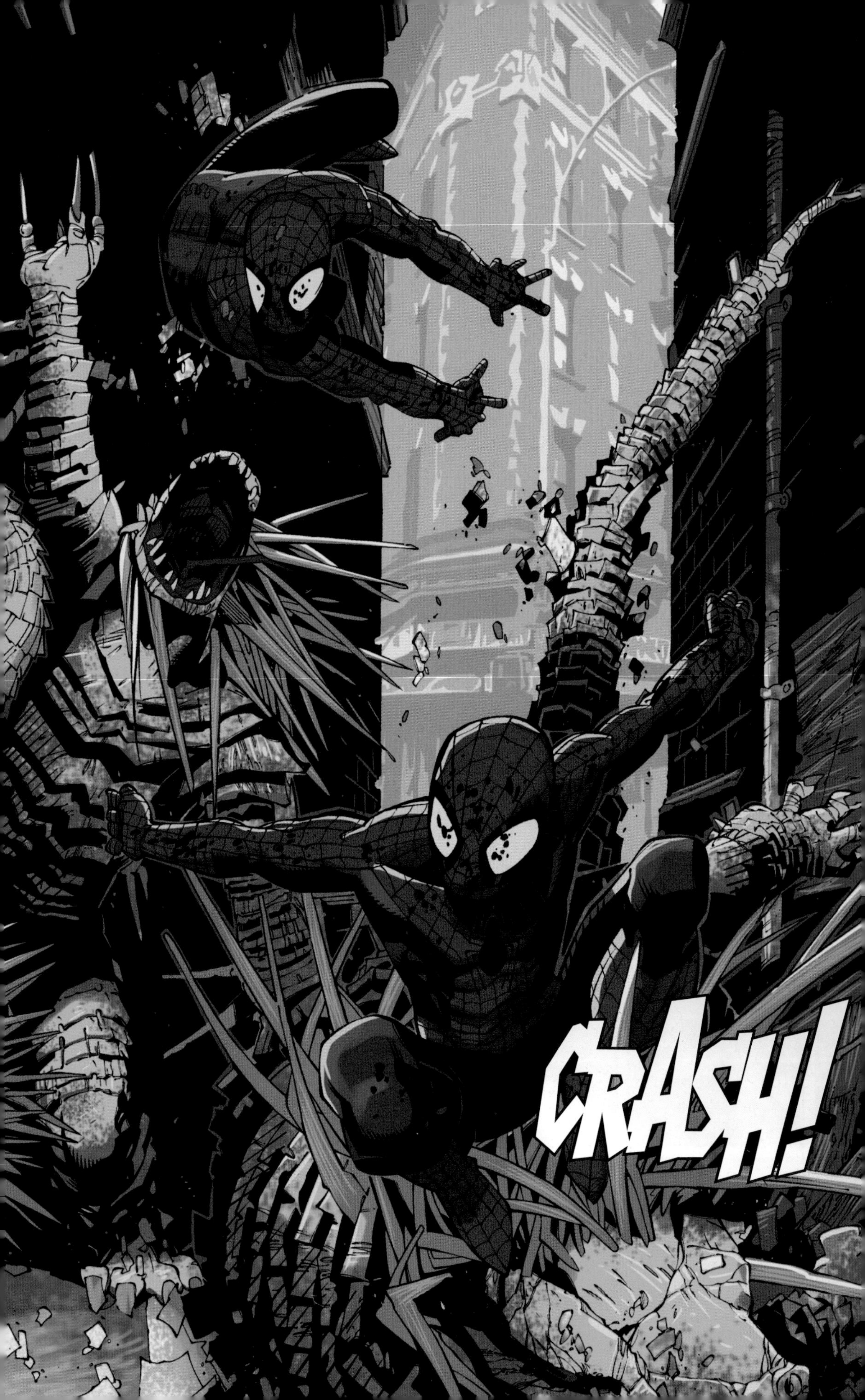
CRASH!

PICTURE IN MY BRAIN.

M-MY HEAD... WHAT'S HE DOING...

MONKEY BRAINS HOLD A LIZARD INSIDE.

TRAPPED, LIKE I WAS TRAPPED.

--URK!

CAN'T MOVE...

DUMB LIZARD ONLY TALK TO LITTLE LIZARDS.

AM SMART LIZARD.

I TALK TO LIZARD INSIDE YOU.

I MAKE LIZARD WAKE UP.

THINK, PETER...

N-NO...I FEEL HIM...

I FEEL HIM IN MY BRAIN...

NO

NO THINK

 NO
THINK ONLY
LOOK

LOOK
CLAWS.

LOOK
TEETH.

LOOK
BLOOD.

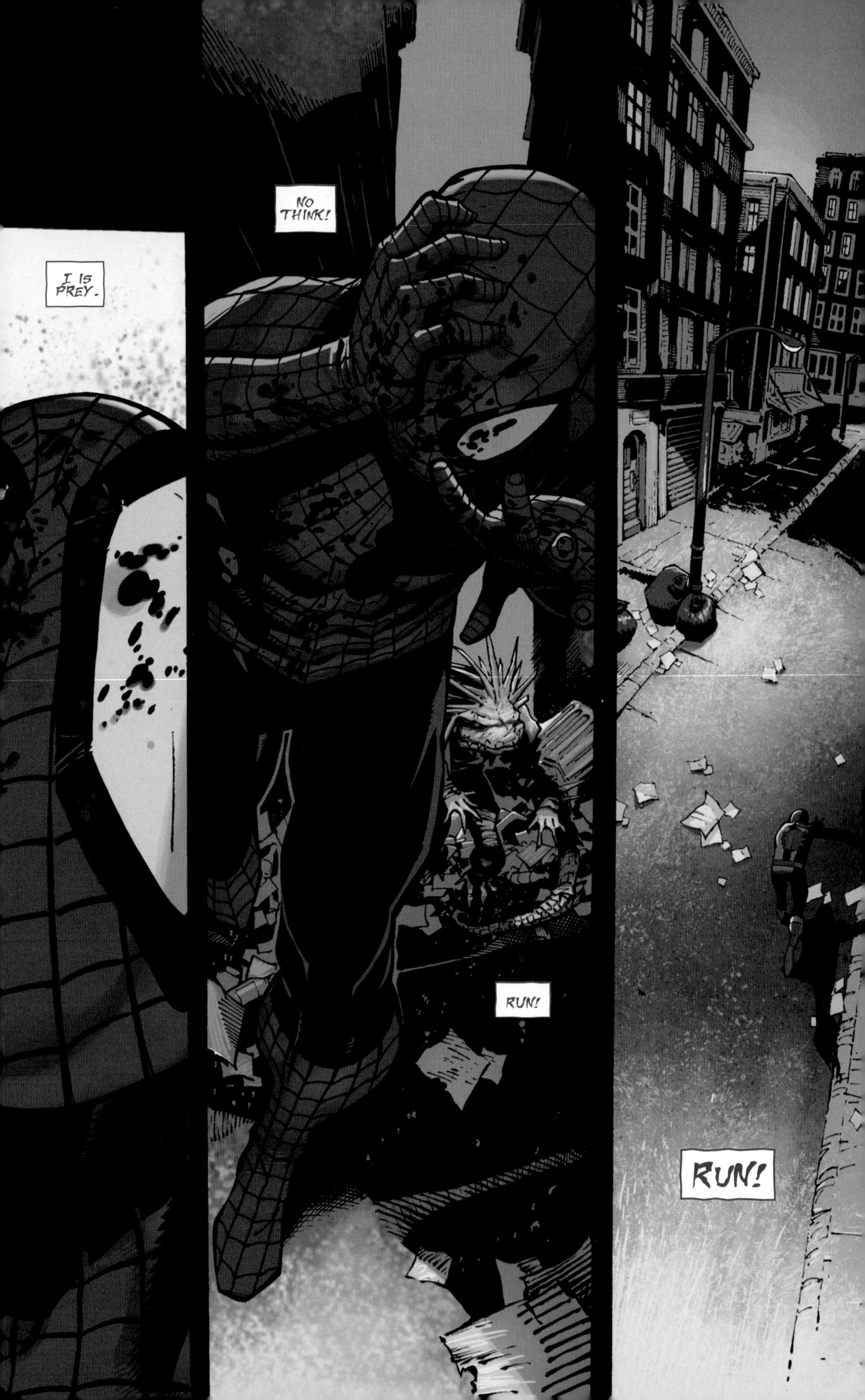
I IS PREY.
NO THINK!
RUN!
RUN!

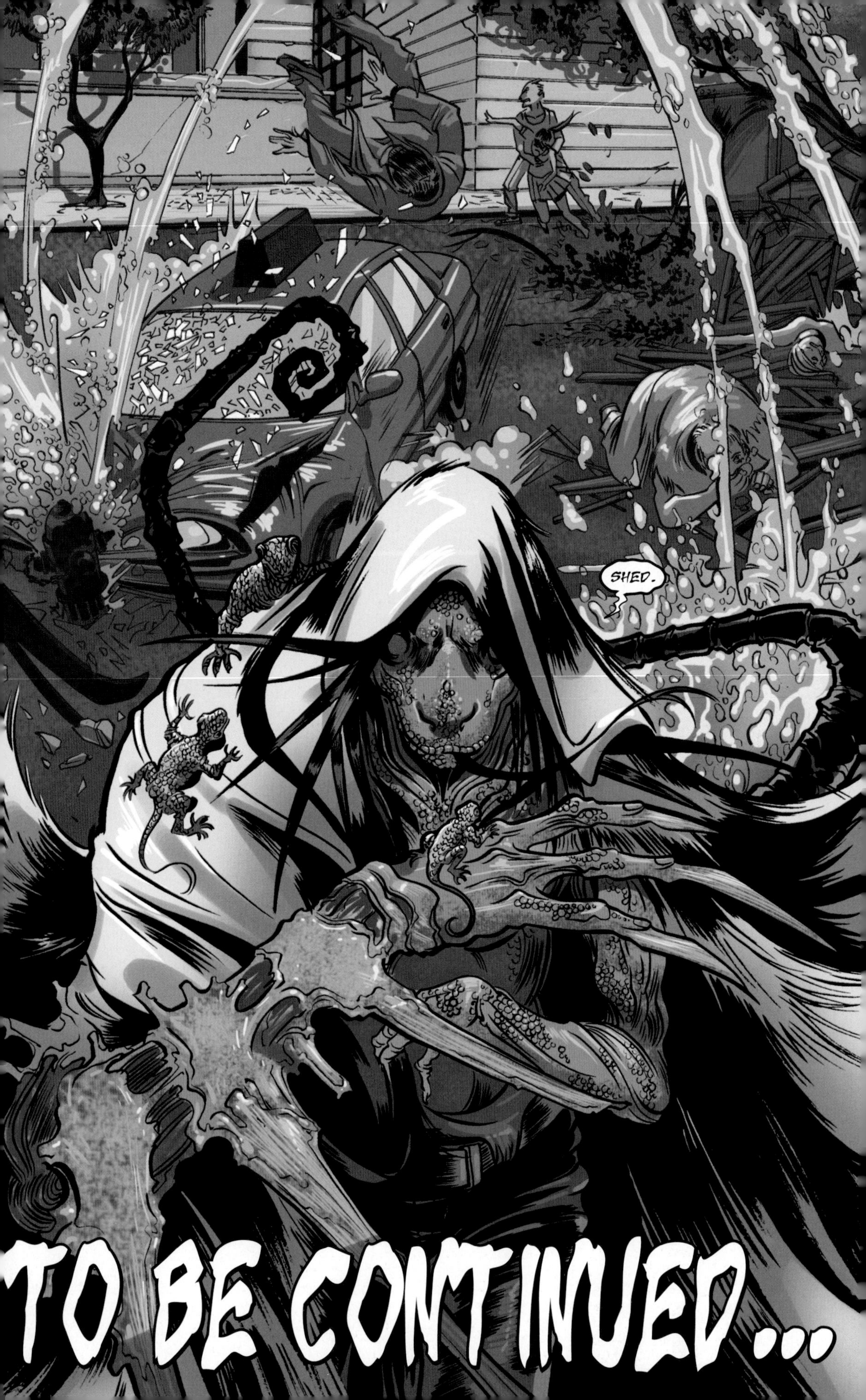
SHED.
TO BE CONTINUED...

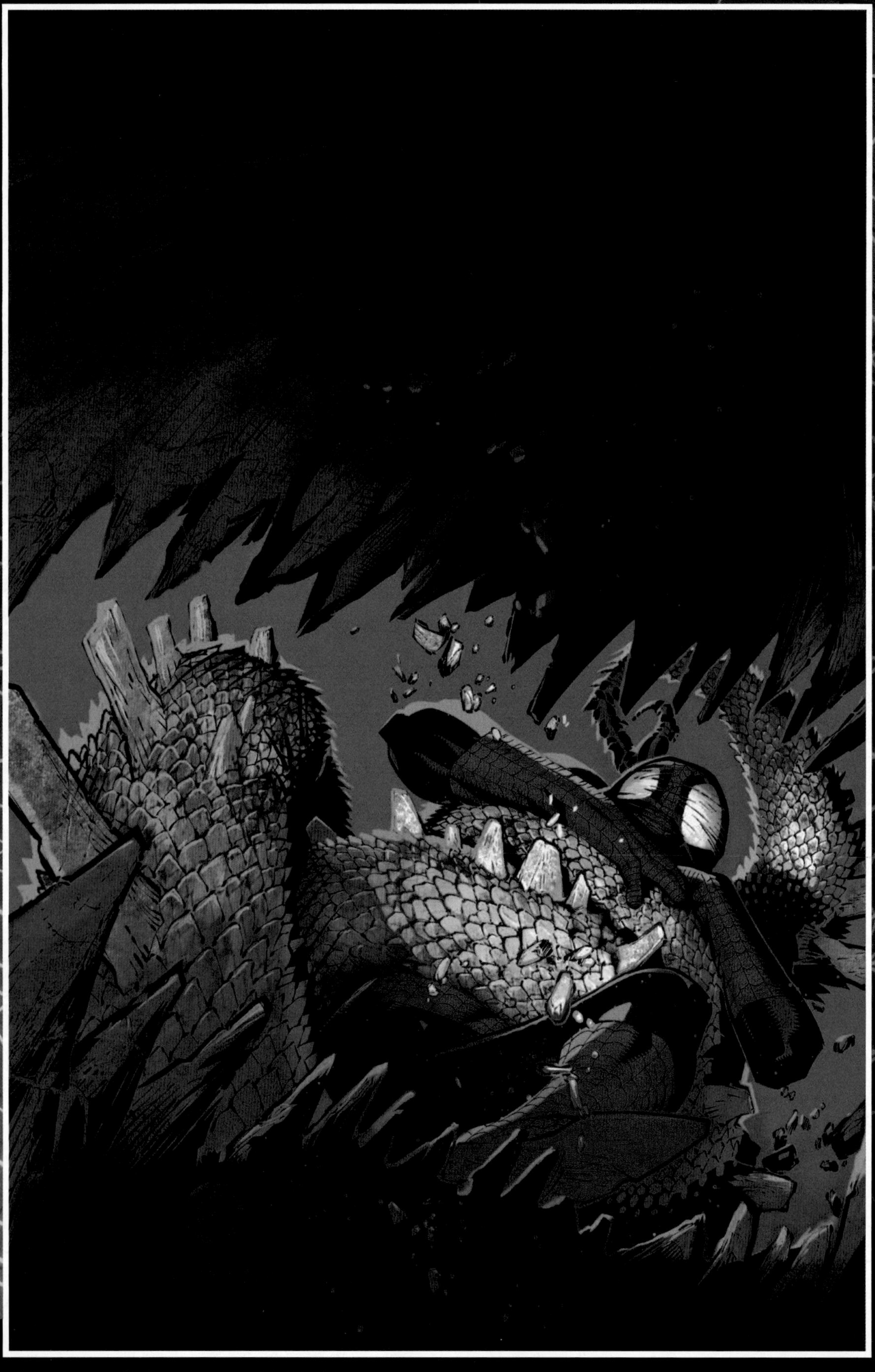

AMAZING SPIDER-MAN #633
COVER BY CHRIS BACHALO & TIM TOWNSEND

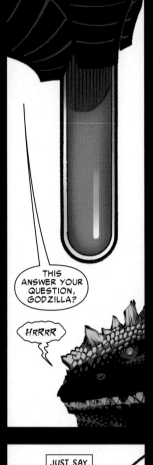

THIS ANSWER YOUR QUESTION, GODZILLA?

HRRRR

THAT'S RIGHT. YOU KNOW.

HARF!

CONNORS WAS USING THIS STUFF TO KEEP HIS REPTILIAN BRAIN LOCKED UP.

IF IT WORKS ON HIM, IT HAS TO WORK ON ME, RIGHT?

PUNT

JUST SAY, "RIGHT."

HARF!

HRRRM...

HARF! HARF!

WHAT IS IT, LITTLE BROTHER?

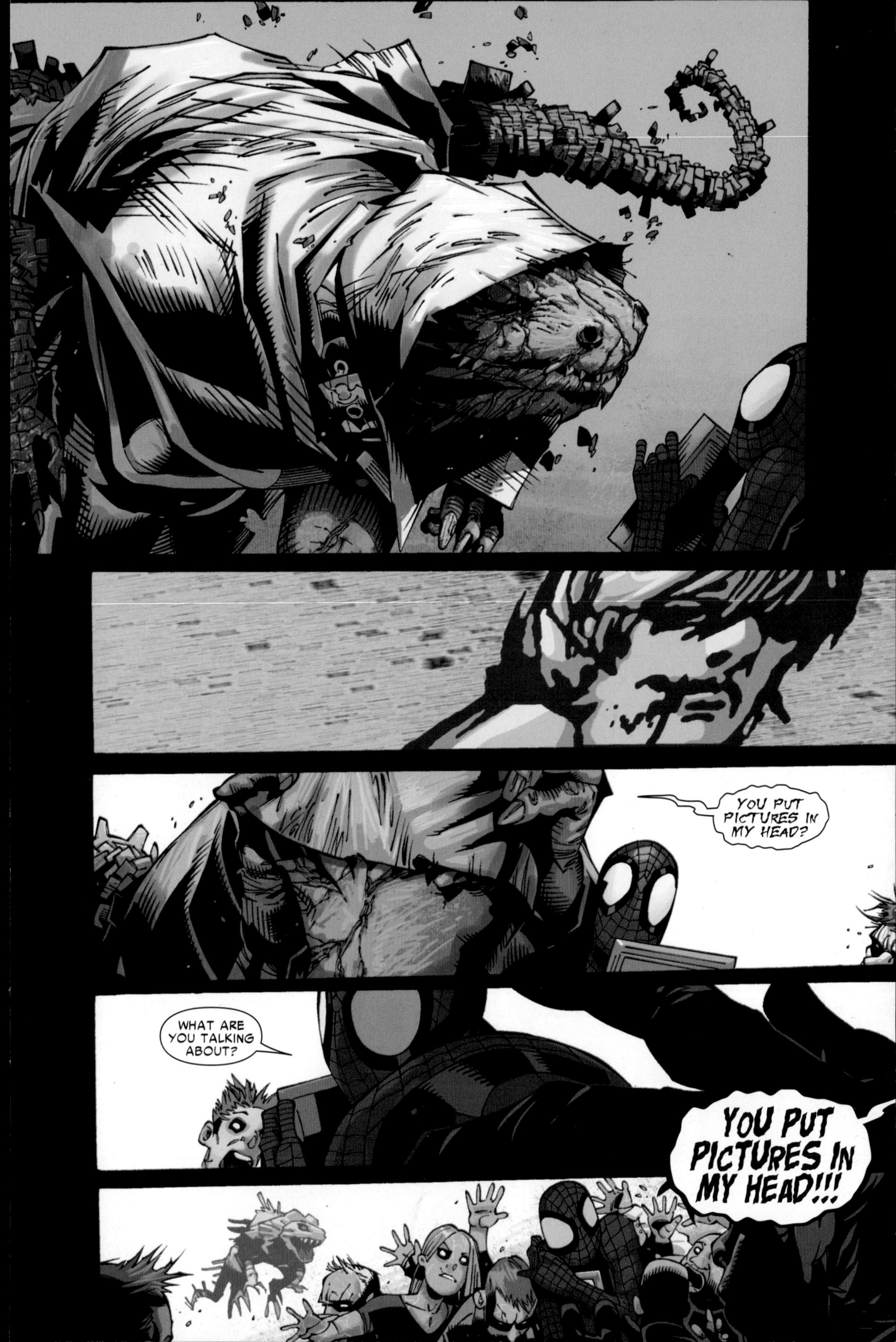
YOU PUT PICTURES IN MY HEAD?
WHAT ARE YOU TALKING ABOUT?
YOU PUT PICTURES IN MY HEAD!!!

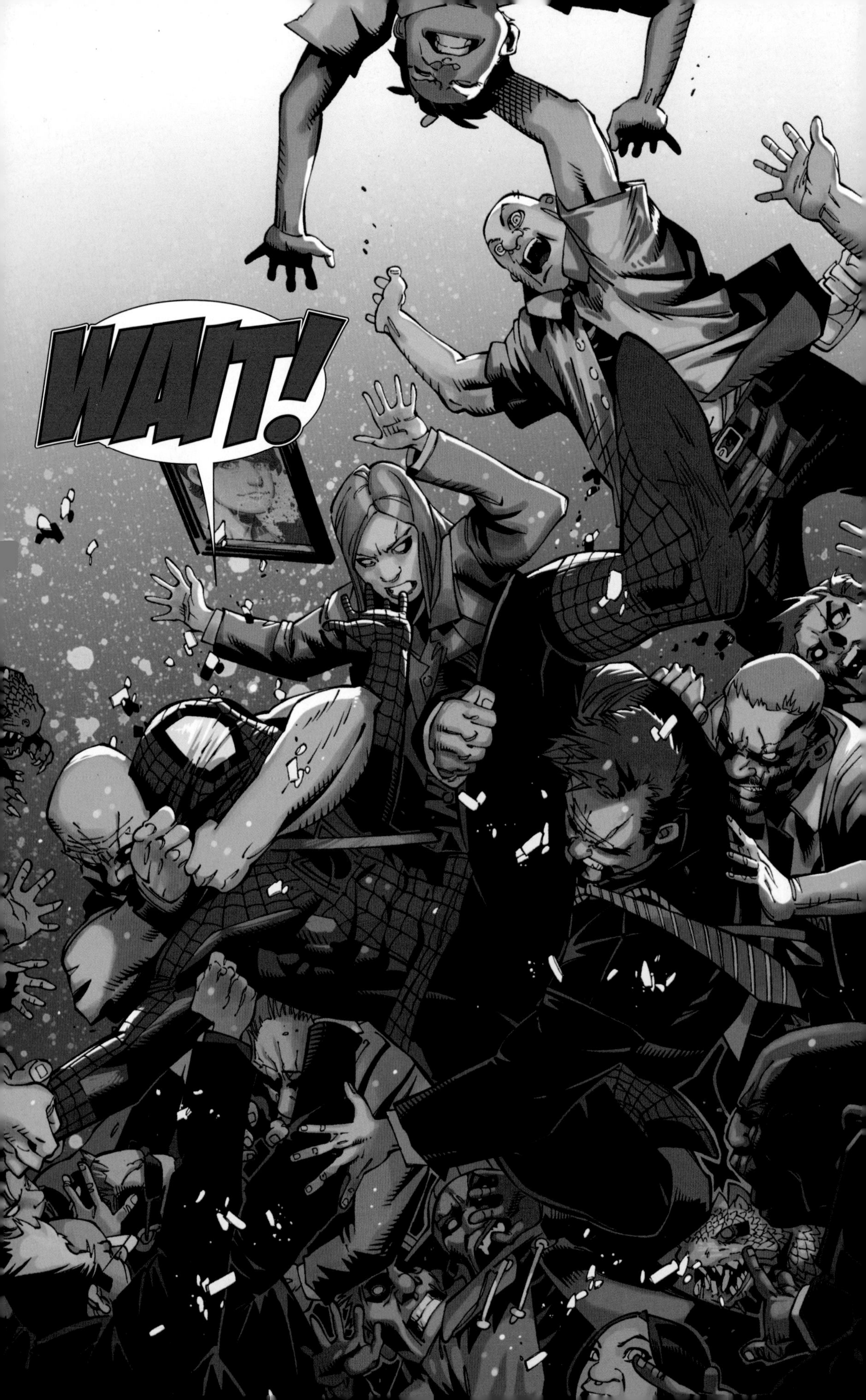
WAIT!

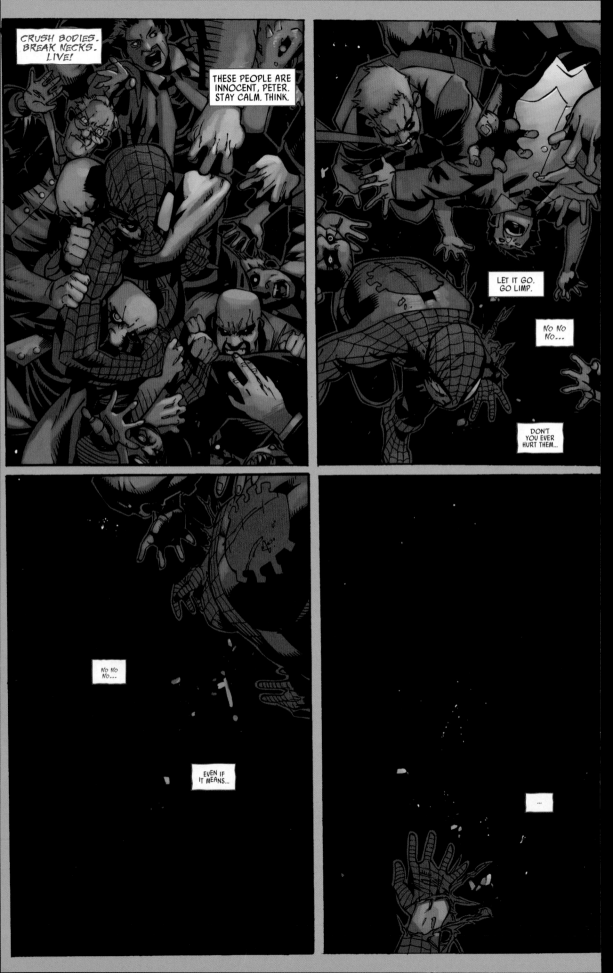

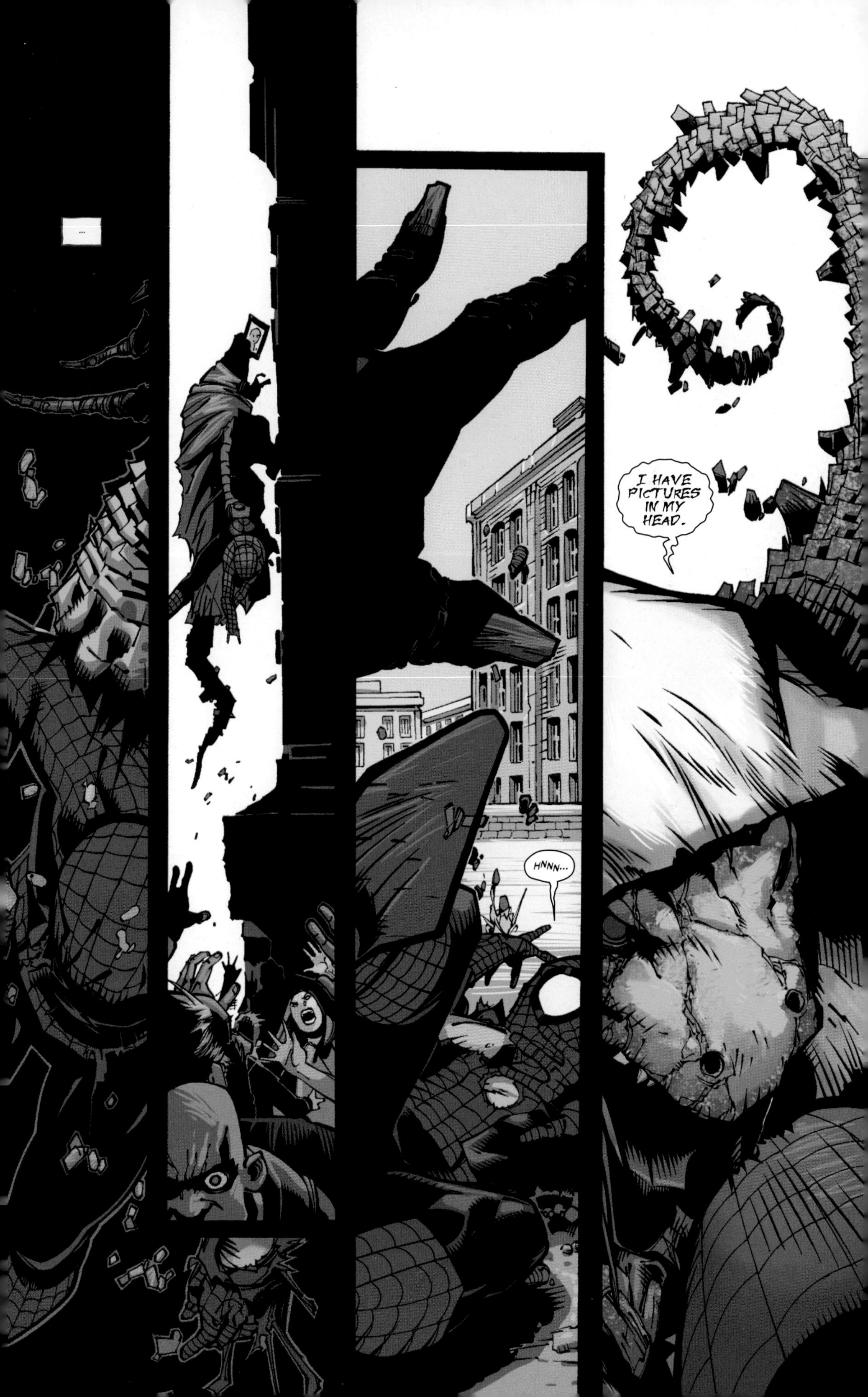
...
I HAVE PICTURES IN MY HEAD.
HNNN...

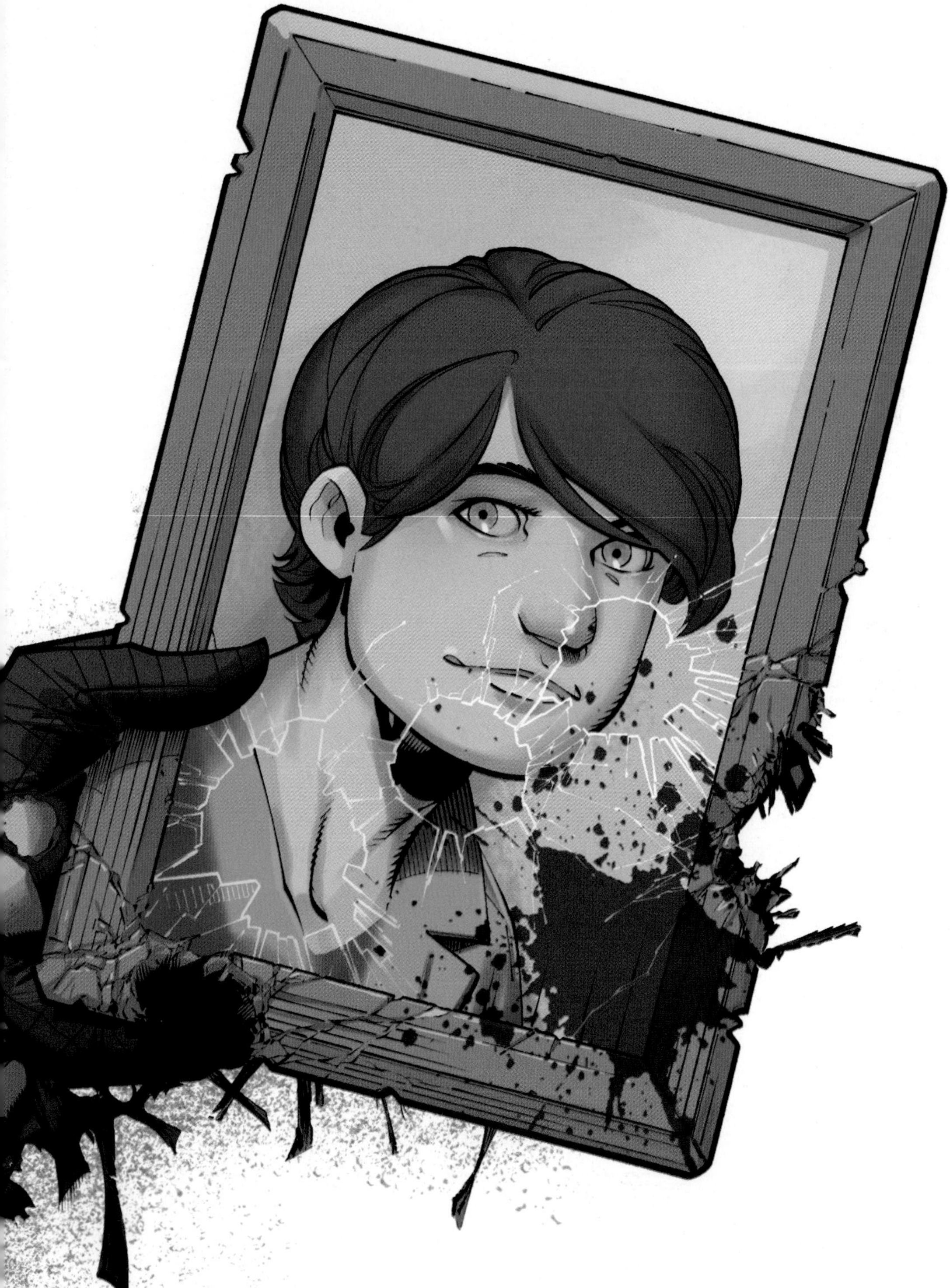

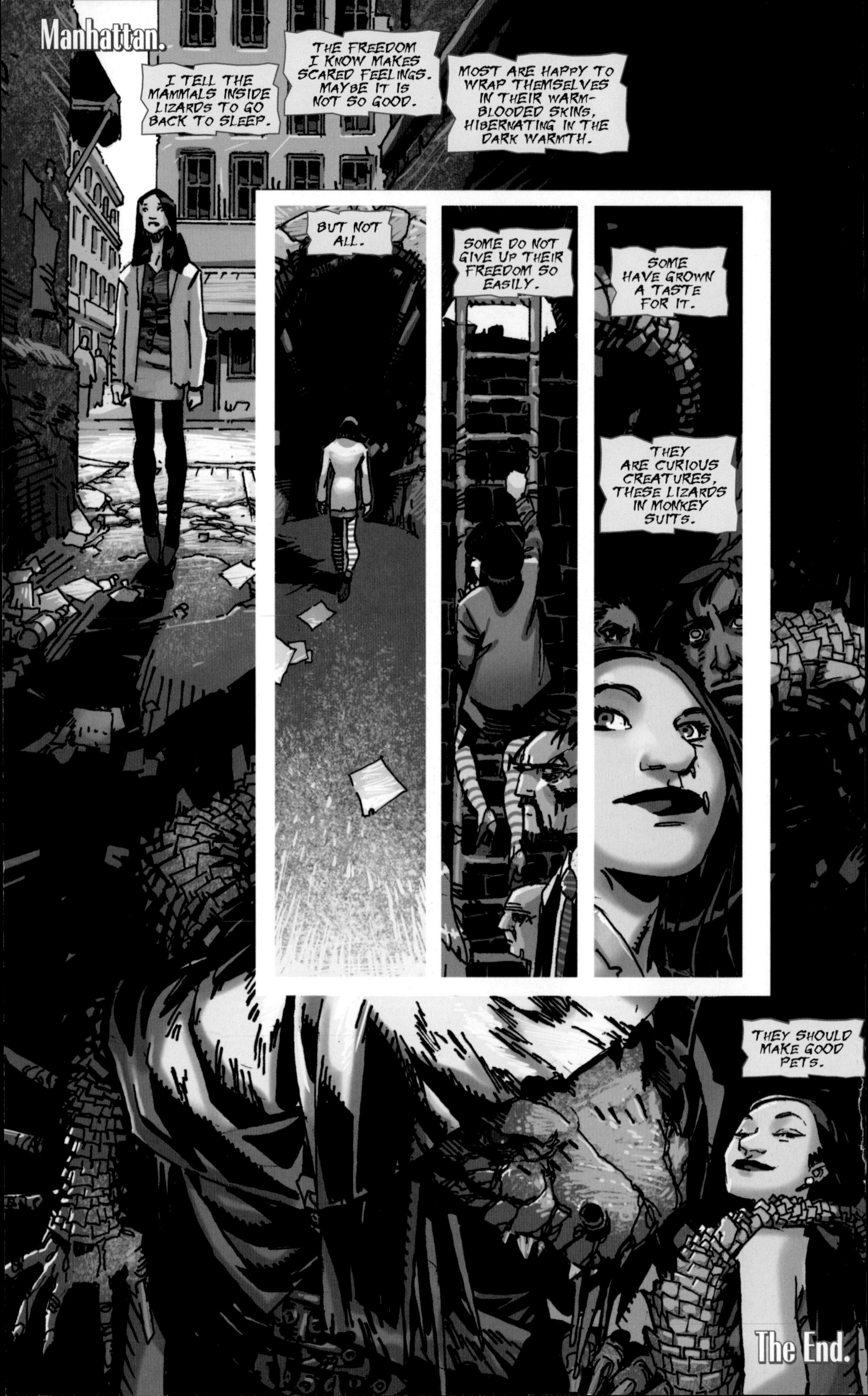

Manhattan.
I TELL THE MAMMALS INSIDE LIZARDS TO GO BACK TO SLEEP.
THE FREEDOM I KNOW MAKES SCARED FEELINGS. MAYBE IT IS NOT SO GOOD.
MOST ARE HAPPY TO WRAP THEMSELVES IN THEIR WARM-BLOODED SKINS, HIBERNATING IN THE DARK WARMTH.
BUT NOT ALL.
SOME DO NOT GIVE UP THEIR FREEDOM SO EASILY.
SOME HAVE GROWN A TASTE FOR IT.
THEY ARE CURIOUS CREATURES, THESE LIZARDS IN MONKEY SUITS.
THEY SHOULD MAKE GOOD PETS.
The End.

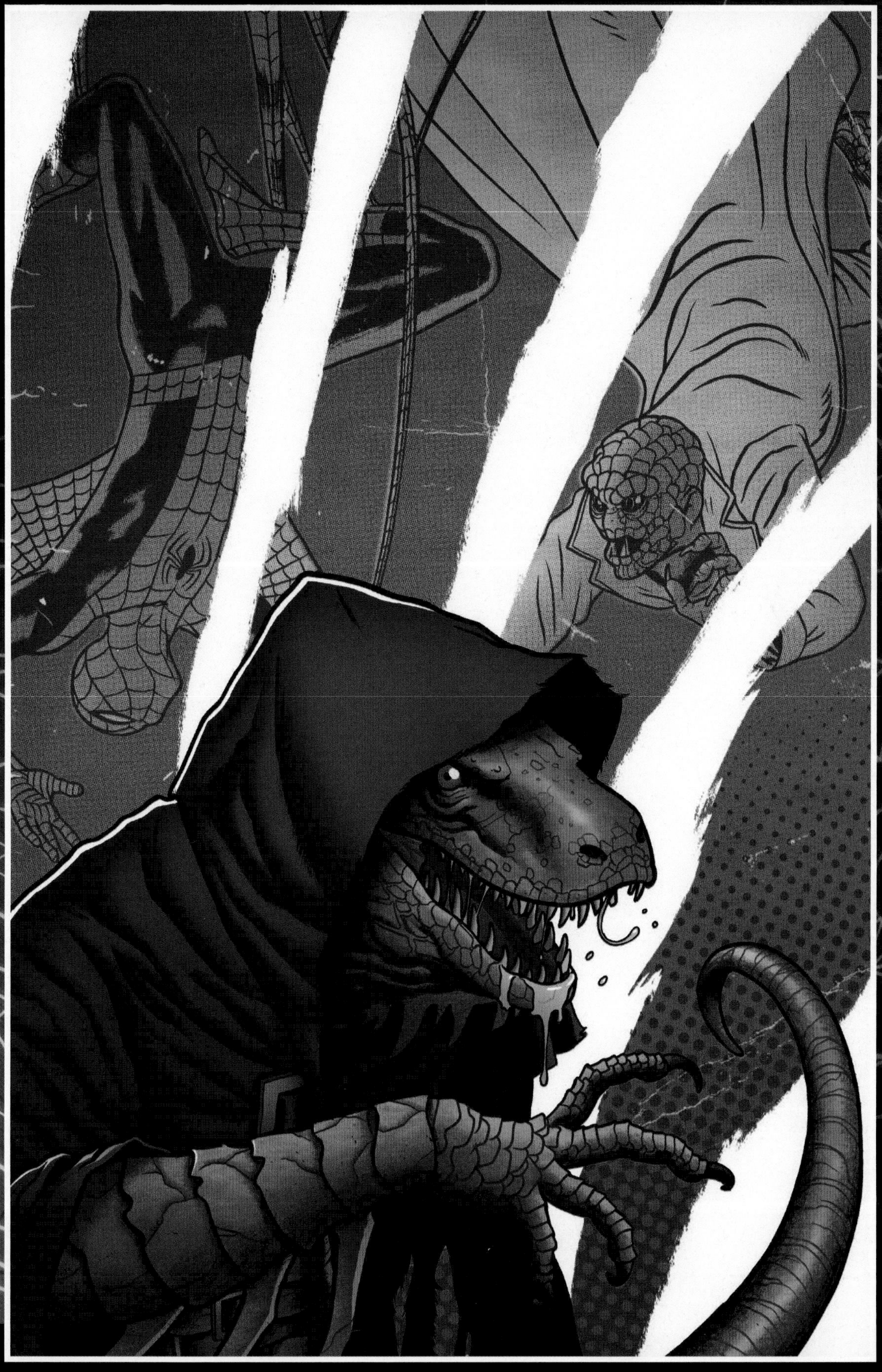

AMAZING SPIDER-MAN #630 VILLAIN VARIANT

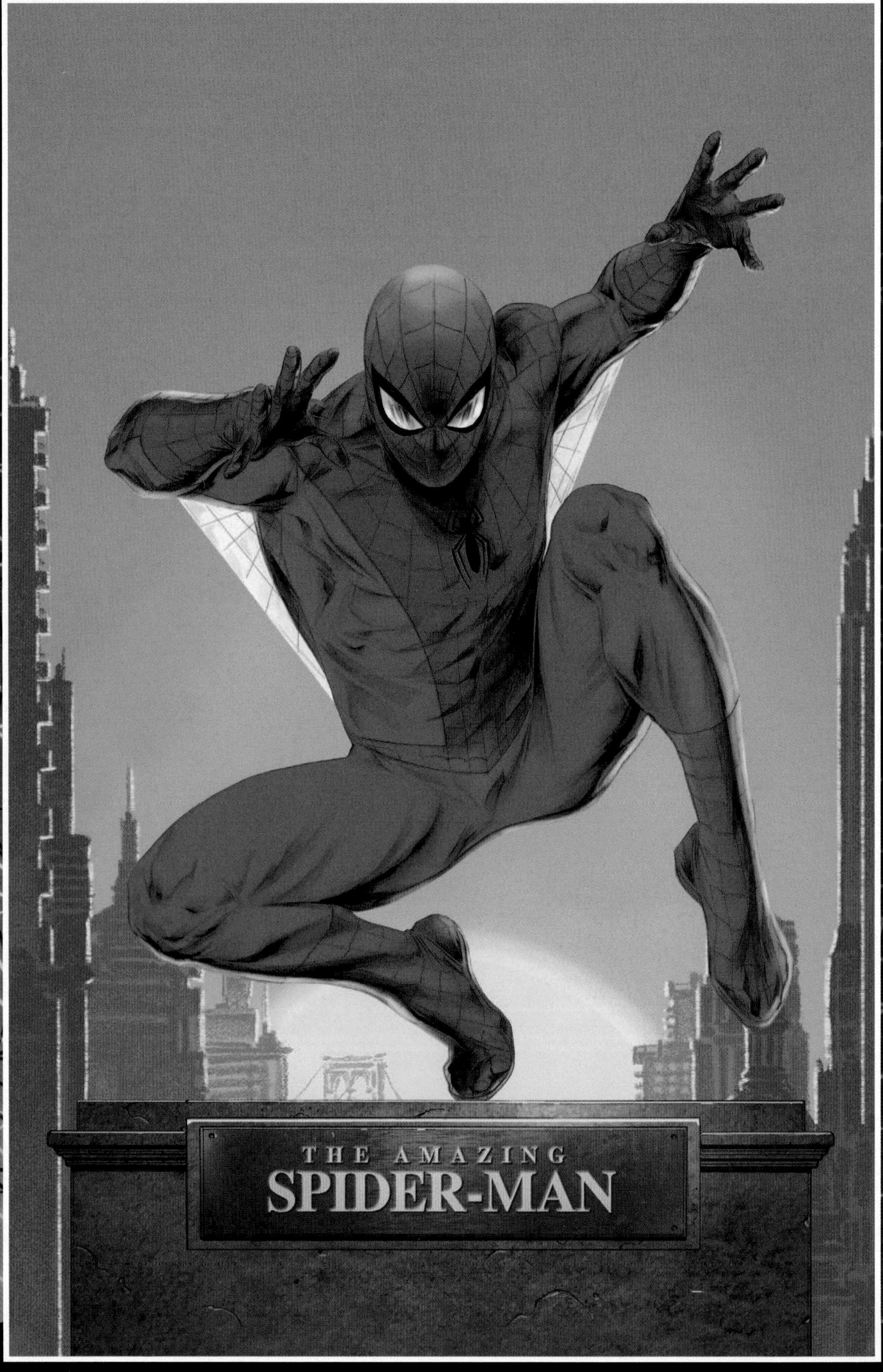
THE AMAZING
SPIDER-MAN

AMAZING SPIDER-MAN #631 HEROIC AGE VARIANT

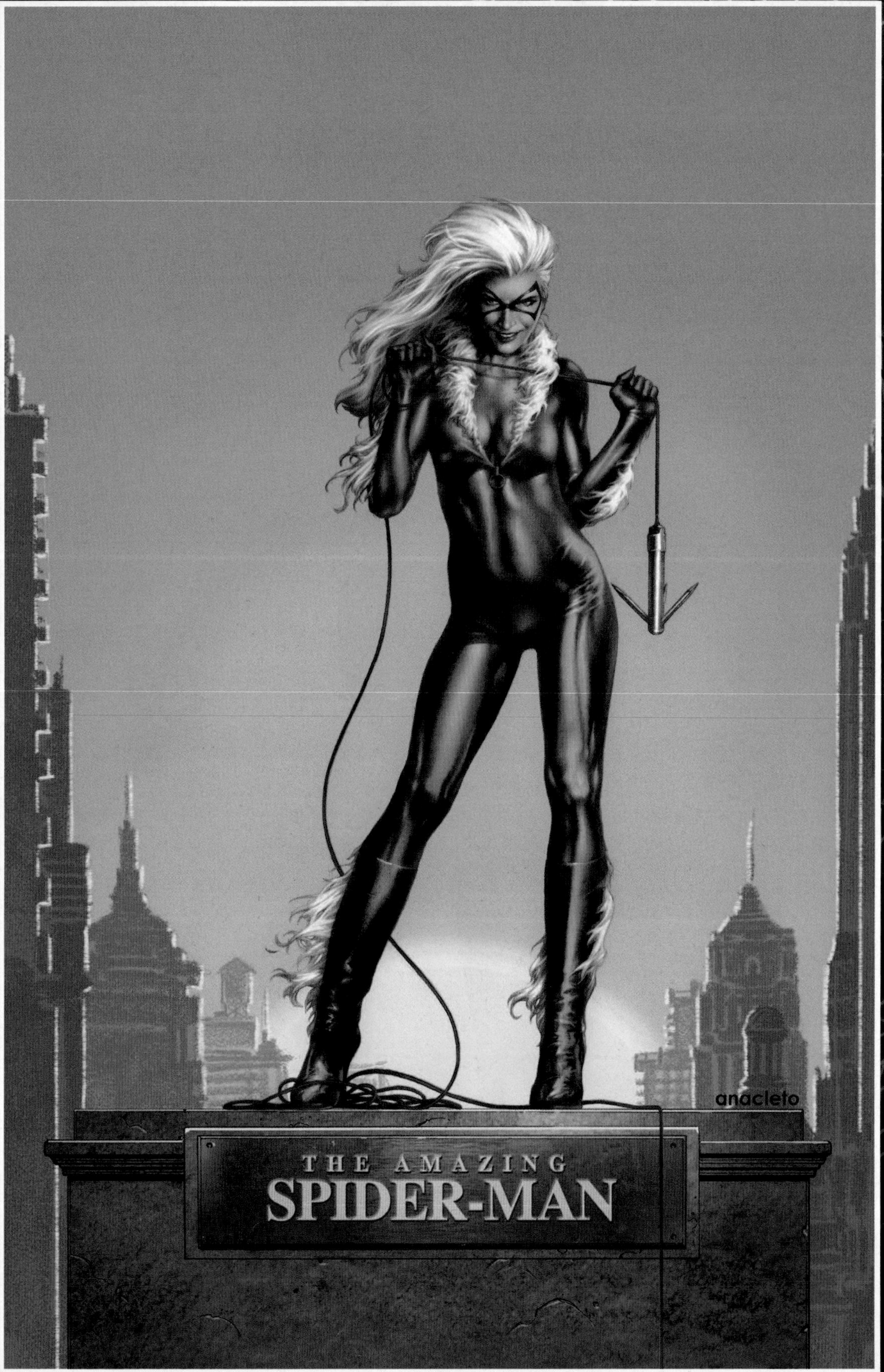
anacleto
THE AMAZING
SPIDER-MAN

AMAZING SPIDER-MAN #632 HEROIC AGE VARIANT
COVER BY JAY ANACLETO & BRIAN HABERLIN

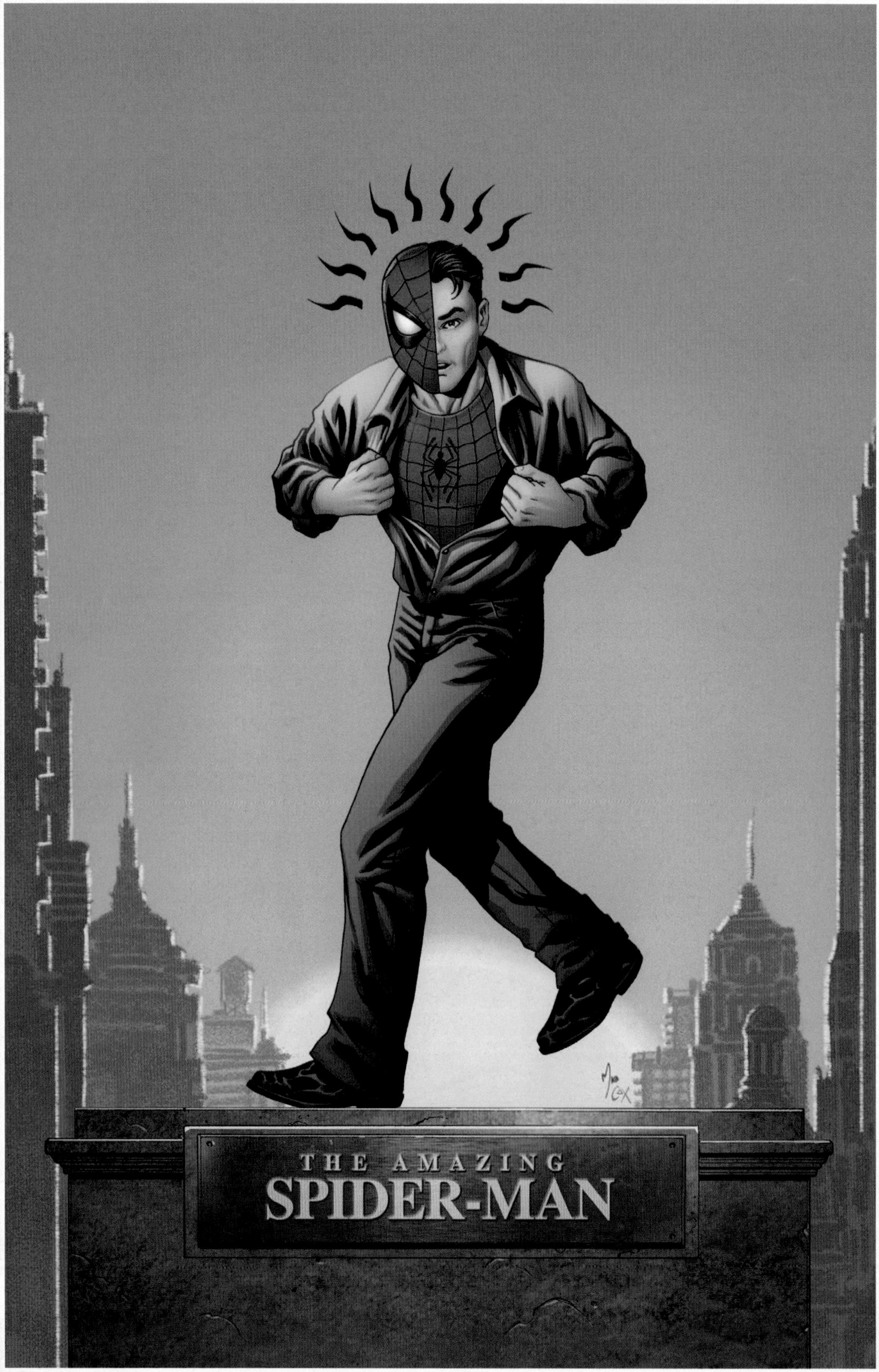
THE AMAZING
SPIDER-MAN

AMAZING SPIDER-MAN #633 HEROIC AGE VARIANT
COVER BY MIKE MCKONE & JEROMY COX

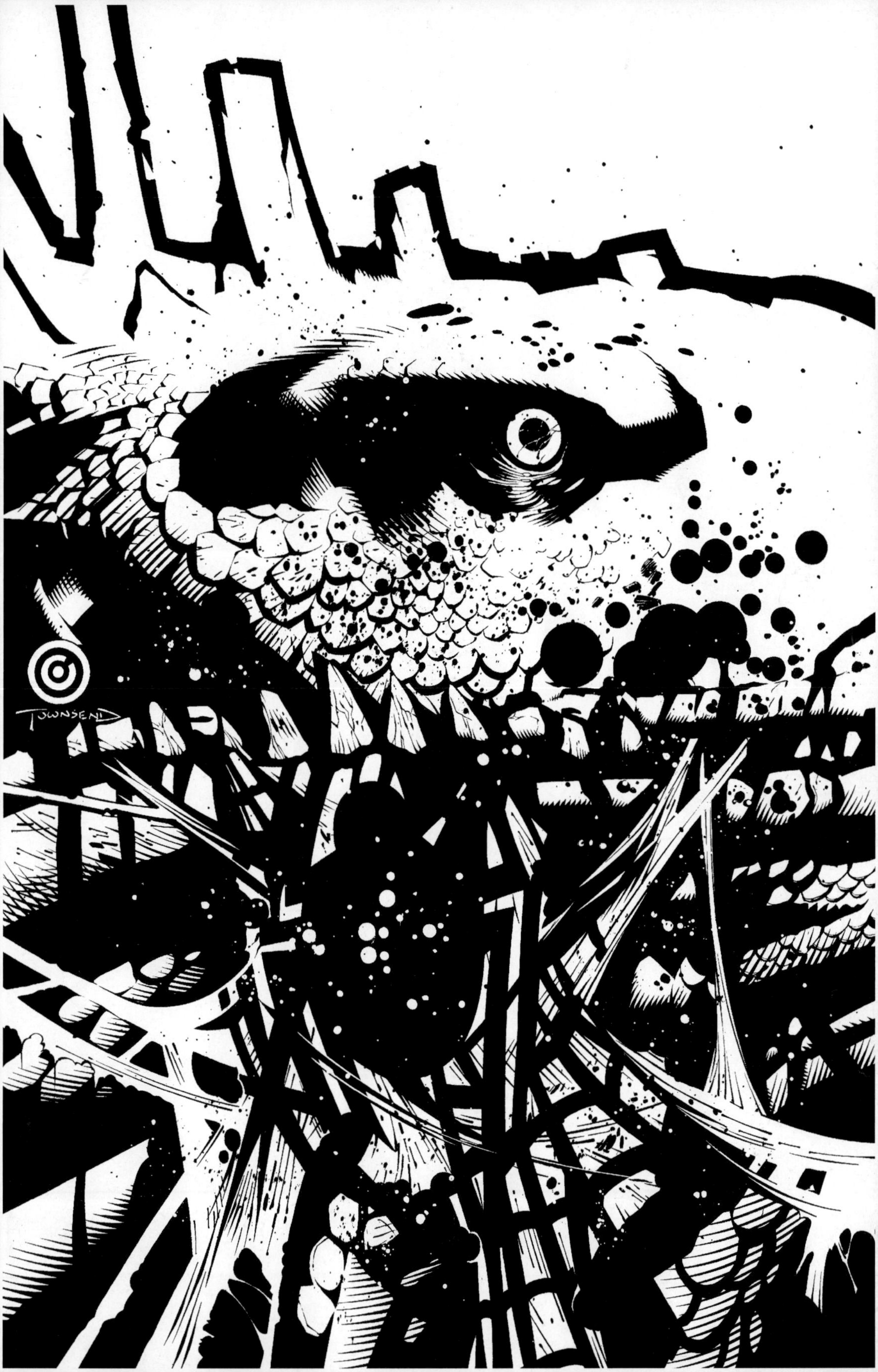
TOWNSEND

AMAZING SPIDER-MAN #630 COVER INKS
BY CHRIS BACHALO & TIM TOWNSEND

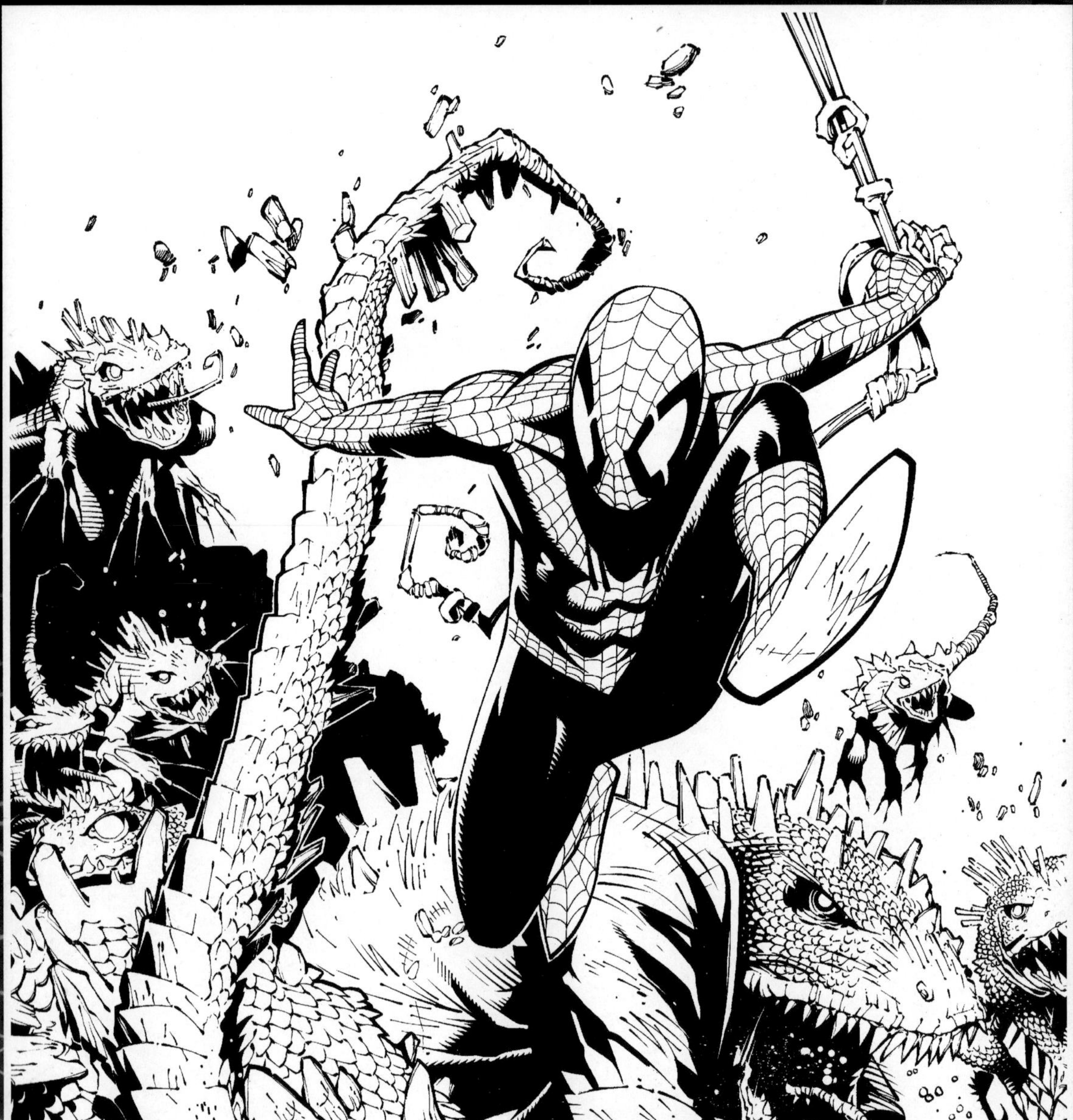
TOWNSEND

AMAZING SPIDER-MAN #631 COVER INKS
BY CHRIS BACHALO & TIM TOWNSEND